Weep with Those Who Weep

A Requiem

Text by Lotta Suter

Music by Robert W. Griffin

Beinn Ard Publishing

Beinn Ard Publishing
Hollis, New Hampshire 03049
www.beinnard.com

ISBN 978-1-889314-66-2 (spiral)
ISBN 978-1-889314-67-9 (paperback)

First edition 2016

Printed in the United States of America

Contents

First Performance

<u>Weep with those who weep: A Requiem</u> was first performed October 2016 at the Edward Pickman Concert Hall of Longy School of Music, Cambridge MA and at the Mason Congregational Church, Mason NH, by the Batraxoi ensemble under the direction of Mark Latham.

Director	Mark Latham
Soprano soloist	Maria Ferrante
Baritone soloist	Donald Wilkinson
Soprano I	Deborah Prince Smith
Soprano I	Lotta Suter
Soprano II	Katheryn Currie
Soprano II	Martha Griffin
Alto	Lisa Mitchell
Alto	Pamela Stevens
Tenor	Jason Wang
Baritone	Garth Griffin
Bass	Robert Griffin
Violin 1	Beth Welty
Violin 2	Harriet Young
Viola	Noralee Walker
Cello	Mark Meess
Double Bass	Anthony Varga
Flute	Rod Ferland
Oboe	Deborah Hencke
Clarinet	Rochelle Goren
Bassoon	Nancy Tong
Trumpet	Rick Bolling
French Horn	Stephen Taylor
Trombone	Eric Saunders
Percussion	Gary Wolpert

Weep With Those Who Weep

A Requiem

The word "requiem" is generally used to describe the Mass for the Dead (Missa pro defunctis) which is similar to a regular Mass except that certain joyful parts are omitted. Requiems have such a rich musical history that the term became – apart from liturgical use - a distinct musical genre for compositions that deal with death and loss. For many centuries the texts of the requiem were sung to Gregorian melodies. In the 16th century individual composers began to set the requiem, a musical tradition that led to several thousand different requiem compositions to this day. Haydn, Mozart, Verdi, Brahms, Dvořák, Fauré, Britten and Rutter, among many others, have written requiems that reflect on death and bereavement.

Many of the composers have used the traditional liturgical form and its Latin words for their work, sometimes omitting one or several movements. Starting in the 18th century and to this day, the requiem has more and more been treated as a concert piece, an oratorio that may be used in funeral services. In the 20th century several requiems were created that dedicated music and words to people killed in wartime or in the Holocaust.

When thinking about creating our own 21st century requiem Weep with Those Who Weep, this librettist had two spiritual ancestors foremost in her mind. The first is Johannes Brahms and his A German Requiem (Ein Deutsches Requiem, ca. 1868) for which the composer did not use the Latin liturgy but assembled words of the Holy Scripture that he himself found especially meaningful. Unlike the traditional Mass for the Dead, Brahms' A German Requiem focuses on the living, beginning the work with the text "Blessed are they that mourn, for they shall be comforted." When he was criticized by contemporaries for not including Christian dogma like "the redeeming death of the Lord", he stated that he was not creating a religious work but addressing mankind. His composition, Brahms insisted, was a "Human Requiem", but he added proudly: "Nevertheless I have my faith."

A second source of inspiration was Benjamin Britten and his War Requiem (1962), which he was commissioned to write for the consecration of the new Coventry Cathedral which had been destroyed in a World War II bombing raid. Britten, an outspoken pacifist, chose to set the traditional Latin Mass for the Dead interwoven with nine poems by the English poet Wilfred Owen who described the horrors of World War I and of every war.

Our new requiem stems not only from experience of personal loss and grief but is also nurtured by the knowledge and certainty that others – like Johannes Brahms and Benjamin Britten - have lost and grieved before us and sought to share their sorrow with those around them. Even before the first word of this requiem was set on paper it was important to be able to "weep with those who weep". As lonely and desperate as the death of a beloved person – or just death itself - can make us feel, we stay connected to all mankind who through the ages and in all places has known growth and decay. To celebrate the community with others is the main intention of Weep with Those Who Weep.

Like the War Requiem, this work contains movements that struggle with "war", with the destructive side of the human species. And like A German Requiem, this libretto is not so certain what God there is to take some of our sins and burdens away. Like the traditional Masses for the Dead, however, we acknowledge that we need liturgy and ceremony to deal with death and loss which are so much more powerful than our individual life. The words and music in this requiem try to reconcile these emotions and thoughts around death using parts of the traditional Mass for the Dead, passages from the Bible and our own contemporary expression of grief and hope.

Following loosely the structure of a traditional requiem, there are seven movements to the piece.

The first movement contains only the traditional words of the Agnus Dei section of the Roman Catholic Mass: "Dona nobis requiem et lux perpetua luceat". It is a plea for peace and light.

The second movement "Eleison", reflecting on the wonders of creation as told to us in the first chapters of Genesis, celebrates our connectedness with nature and the people around us: "Rejoice with those who rejoice and weep with those who weep" (Romans 12:15).

The third movement "Dies Irae" is a long and at times angry lament about death and destruction. We weep for the natural deaths and the shameful deaths that we humans ourselves cause so that lives are ended before their time. In our own words we name the destruction of our way of life on this planet. The elegy ends with the liturgical words (set in Latin): "That day of tears and mourning, when from the ashes shall arise all humanity to be judged."

In the fourth movement we sink to a "bottomless pit" of despair where the many deaths become one darkness, one stillness, one death. Even our own individual words fail us and all that is left is the desperate plea from the Mass of the Dead: "Deliver us from the jaws of the lion and let us not fall into darkness."

The fifth movement is named "Hosanna in excelsis". It is not a loud jubilation, but a first glimpse of hope: "When we weep again begins the resurrection."

The sixth movement "Qui tollit peccata mundi?" reflects on the words of the Agnus Dei. We talk about the possibility that there is no certain God, no Agnus Dei to carry our sins and burdens. Can we go on just with the faith in ourselves and in each other, and still accept the world "in full magnitude"?

The last movement "Lux perpetua" combines the sentiment and the words of the two first movements. After having gone through this haunting process of grief we might perceive our connectedness to the world around us and to our fellow human beings even more intensely. And we repeat our plea, humbly but full of hope: "Dona nobis requiem et lux perpetua luceat."

The music of <u>Weep with Those Who Weep</u>, across its broad spectrum of moods and tonalities, reflects this progression of descent and ascent expressed in the text. The first movement, opening with a long, somber melody in the oboe, has a yearning and introspective character that continues into the second movement. The music of the third and fourth movements descends into a more agitated and conflicted realm of anger and judgement. With the fifth movement, the requiem enters a quieter mood, moving upward through the doubts of the sixth movement to return at last in the final movement to the long melodic themes with which the requiem began,

This overall organization is reflected in the harmonic structure of the requiem, which moves downward by thirds for the first four movements, then upwards by thirds through the final movement:

Movement 1 (Dona nobis requiem): B-minor
Movement 2 (Eleison): G-minor
Movement 3 (Dies Irae): E-minor
Movement 4 (De profundo lacu): C-minor
Movement 5 (Hosanna in excelsis): E-flat major
Movement 6 (Qui tollit peccata mundi?): G-minor
Movement 7 (Lux perpetua): B-minor): D-major

A similar A-B-A harmonic structure, starting in B-minor, dropping to F-minor and then returning to B-minor, characterizes the first movement, which serves as a prelude to the other six movements. This structure is also reflected in the thematic structure of the first movement:

A: Instrumental theme (oboe solo)
B: Chorus (tenors only) statement of "Dona nobis requiem" melody
C: Choral fugue on "Dona nobis requiem"
B: Chorus (all parts) restatement of "Dona nobis requiem" melody
A: Instrumental restatement of initial oboe solo

The final movement uses a similar but enlarged A-B-A structure both harmonically and thematically.

A: Eleison (B-minor)
B: Instrumental flute solo (E-minor)
C: Fugato on "Weep we shall" (B-minor)
D: Choral reprise of "With all animals" from movement 2 (B-minor)
E: Choral reprise of "by day and night" from movement 2 (E-minor)
F: Dona nobis requiem (derived Eleison of part A) (B-minor)

The alternation of B-minor and E-minor in this movement is also a reflection of a similar alternating structure in other movements, especially movements 3, 4 and 5. In movement 3 ("Dies Irae"), the instrumental and choral setting of the words "Dies Irae", set in an agitated 7/8 meter in which dissonant, rising chords are punctuated by pounding rhythm in the timpani, separates each of the verses. In movement 4 ("De profundo lacu"), the verses are separated by the "De poenis", which increases in intensity and volume with each iteration until the final statement explodes in an agonized plea to "deliver us from the jaws of the lion". Movement 5 ("Hosanna in excelsis") alternates between verses sung by the chorus and the "Hosanna" refrain sung by the soprano soloist.

Movements 2 and 6 reflect both the cyclic structure of the first and last movements and the verse-chorus structure of the middle movements. Movement 2 begins with a viola solo, followed by the choral setting of "In heaven and on earth"; the viola solo then returns, followed by the choral setting of "We will weep / eleison". This alternating structure ends, however, with a short coda that returns to a shortened echo of the viola solo. Similarly, movement 6 begins with a violin solo, followed by the soprano solo on "Agnus dei"; the violin solo returns, followed by the choral setting of "And if there is no sacrificial lamb / Qui tollis". Once again, the alternating structure ends with a short coda that returns to the violin solo.

As already indicated by the viola and violin solos of these two movements, each movement reflects the larger descent/ascent structure of the requiem in the timbre of its solo instrument.

Movement 1 (Dona nobis requiem): oboe solo
Movement 2 (Eleison): viola solo
Movement 3 (Dies Irae): timpani solo

Movement 4 (De profundo lacu): cello solo
Movement 5 (Hosanna in excelsis): clarinet solo
Movement 6 (Qui tollit peccata mundi): violin solo
Movement 7 (Lux perpetua): B-minor): flute solo

The timbre defined by these solos, however, also varies considerably within each movement. The orchestra takes advantage of four instrumental families: strings, woodwinds, brass and percussion. In some cases, a movement uses these instrumental families in contrast to each other, such as in the string ensemble of "In heaven" and the woodwind setting of "Under trees" in movement 2. In other cases, instruments are combined to create unusual tonalities, such as the woodwind/contrabass/timpani orchestration underlying the baritone solos in movement 3. The full orchestra is used a number of times, particularly in "we will rejoice" in movement 2, as well as at the end of the requiem.

The requiem uses many different vocal ensembles to express the texts. The soprano and baritone solos of movements 3 through 6 reflect the more individual voices of their texts, such as in the baritone's lament for human cruelty and ignorance in movement 3. The more communal statements, such as the plea "Dona nobis requiem", are set both in unison singing by individual parts, such as the initial melody on "Dona nobis" by the tenors in movement 1, and in both homophonic and polyphonic singing by four-, five- and six-part chorus. The entire vocal ensemble of soloists and chorus joins together in movement 7 in the final 6-voice statement of "Et lux perpetua luceat", as does the entire orchestra in the final coda.

The diversity of timbre, rhythm and ensemble is counter-balanced by various unifying elements in the music, similar to the unifying repetition of "Dona nobis requiem" and "Eleison" in the text. The most important of these unifying elements is the short motif first voiced in the oboe solo at the start of the piece. The motif consists of a 4-note descending phrase (C#-B-A-G), in which the last two notes are transposed up an octave to create the interval of a seventh between the second and third notes. This same motif occurs in some form at the start of each movement:

Movement 1; statement of motif in first four notes of oboe solo
Movement 2: descending 4-note motif in first measure of viola solo
Movement 3: descending 4th in first measure of orchestra
Movement 4: descending 4-note motif in first and second measure of cello solo
Movement 5: statement of motif in second measure of introduction
Movement 6; statement of motif in first four notes of violin solo
Movement 7: statement of motif in second measure of flute solo

Similarly, the descending 4-note motif is used to construct the fugatos on "We will weep" in movement 2 and "Weep we shall" in movement 7, the fugue theme in movement 1 and the alto/tenor 4-note motifs in the "Sale nobis" and "Lacrimosa" in movement 3.

The music of <u>Weep with Those Who Weep</u> is enriched by allusions to other works. The most explicit allusion is the statement of the plainsong "Veni creator spiritus" ("Come, creator spirit") by the French horn in the final section of movement 4 ("De profundo lacu"). The evocation of this ancient prayer is a reminder of the universality of the grief that is the focus of the requiem.

Throughout the music of <u>Weep with Those Who Weep</u> there are echoes of other requiems, especially of Brahms' <u>A German Requiem.</u> For example, the baritone solo in the third movement of Brahms' requiem and in the third movement of <u>Weep with Those Who Weep</u> is set above a quarter-note syncopated rhythm in the bass (in 4/4 in the Brahms, in 7/4 in "<u>Weep with Those Who Weep</u>). There are also numerous echoes of Brahms' orchestration, such as the use of triplets in the second movements of both requiems and the arpeggio accompaniments in their first movements.

Above all, like the music of Brahms' requiem, the music of <u>Weep with Those Who Weep</u> represents a very personal response to human mortality: to the deaths of those we love and to the death that each of us must face. At the same time, in the music as in the words, we have tried to express the commonality that we share in the face of tragedy, the community that we participate in when we weep with those who weep and rejoice with those who rejoice.

Weep with Those Who Weep
A Requiem

I. Dona nobis requiem

Dona nobis requiem
et lux perpetua luceat

II Eleison

In heaven and on earth,
by day and night
on high seas and in deep dales
under trees and in the open
in glaring sun and under a silent moon,
with every bird and fish,
with all animals, both tamed and wild,
we will rejoice with those who rejoice
and weep with those who weep.
We will weep with those who weep.
Eleison, eleison, eleison.

III Dies Irae

We weep
for the death that is in store for all of us
and for the deaths we have lived to see
in the passing of our friends and kin
our brothers and sisters,
our parents and children -
the mortality of our children most of all
fills us with deadly fear.
Sale nobis, fons pietatis.

We weep over the tragic deaths
in natural disasters
and over the shameful deaths
of our disastrous human history,
in which to this day
again and again
lives are ended before their time.
Dies irae, dies illa.
solvet saeclum in favilla.

Men, women and children
are killed
for the color of their skin,
for their gender
for their faith -
even for their faith in a just and reasonable world -
for their origin
for their poverty
- which by itself is deadly.

They perish
locked in prisons and working plants
exposed to open seas and in torrid deserts
slaughtered in eternal wars
ripped apart by robot devices
exiled in unknown lands
which do not welcome them,
or tied to a place,
that cannot give them life..

To this day
time and again
and in all places
there are master races,
who arrogate the right
to rule over life and death
of other human beings
in that short time
before their own demise.

And as a human species
we subdue the whole earth.
We set the odds
for the butterfly to survive
in the genetically altered monoculture.
We decide which plants and animals must die
before their time.
Dies irae, dies illa
solvet saeclum in favilla.

Donum fac remissionis
ante diem rationis.
We destroy
the world

because that is easier
and more convenient
than to save the world
time and again
and in all places.

And then we beweep
dwindling glaciers
bloated deserts
eroded hills
cut-down forests
polluted waters
contaminated soils
as if we were victims
of a force majeure.

We have barely any tears left
For transience itself,
which used to touch us
in the death of a common fly
or the fall of a fledgling
from its high nest.
Or when the mountain stream
carried off scree and pebbles
and filled up the lake
that we children wished to be
ever big and blue
and everlasting.

Tearless we go on weeping
for the deaths we have lived to see
and for the death
that is in store for us all.
Lacrimosa dies illa
qua resurget ex favilla
judicandus homo reus.

IV De profundo lacu

We weep
until deep in the night
the many deaths condense
into the one dark death,
whose blackness swallows all.

De poenis inferni
et de profundo lacu
"miserere!" supplicamus
libera nos de ore leonis
ne cadamus in obscurum.

No light
pierces the gloom.
No sun nor moon
shines into
the bottomless pit.

De poenis inferni
et de profundo lacu
"miserere!" supplicamus
libera nos de ore leonis
ne cadamus in obscurum.

No life
pulses in the solid blackness.
No flapping wing
moves
the empty air.

De poenis inferni
et de profundo lacu
"miserere!" supplicamus
libera nos de ore leonis
ne cadamus in obscurum.

Neither faith nor hope
survive in such deepness.
Rare is the love
that dares to go
so far, so low.

De poenis inferni
et de profundo lacu
"miserere!" supplicamus
libera nos de ore leonis
ne cadamus in obscurum.

And thus we plead
in our despair for deliverance
from our agonies
there in the depth where seaweeds
strangle our soul.

De poenis inferni
et de profundo lacu
"miserere!" supplicamus
libera nos de ore leonis
ne cadamus in obscurum.

We cry to God,
to our mothers,
to life itself:
Deliver us from the jaws of the lion
and let us not fall into darkness!

V Hosanna in excelsis

When we may weep again
begins the resurrection.
Hosanna in excelsis!

When we weep
we can return to life.
Hosanna in excelsis!
When we weep with those who weep,
those who rejoice will give us joy.
Hosanna in excelsis!

Pleni sunt coeli et terra
gloria magnifica
Hosanna in excelsis!

VI Qui tollit peccata mundi?

Agnus Dei, qui tollis
peccata mundi,
dona nobis requiem.

And if there is no sacrificial lamb
to take on the sins of the world
and give us everlasting peace?

If there is none but we,
the weeping and the rejoicing
and the faith in our gracious bond?

Will we find ease
in ourselves, in others
in the world we have created?

Are we ready to accept
its blame and beauty
in full magnitude?

Qui tollit peccata mundi?
Dona nobis requiem.

VII Lux perpetua

Eleison, eleison, eleison.
Weep we shall with those who weep
and rejoice with the joyful.
With those who rejoice we shall rejoice,
with all animals both tamed and wild
with every bird and fish,
in glaring sun and under a silent moon,
under trees and in the open
on high seas and in deep dales
by day and night
on earth and in heaven.
Dona nobis requiem
et lux perpetua luceat.

I. Dona nobis requiem

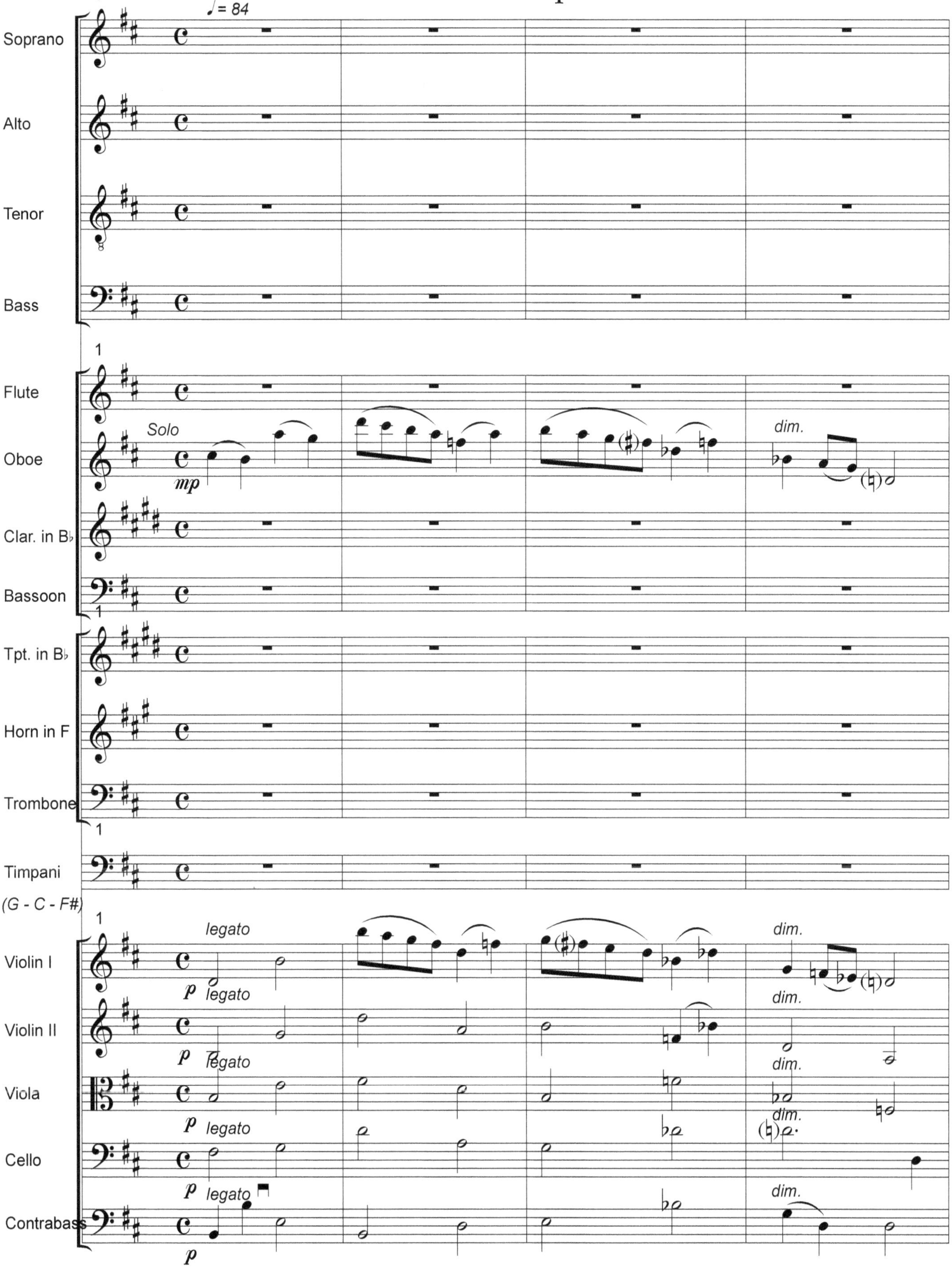

5
Sop
Alto
Ten
Bass
5
Fl.
Ob.
p
B♭ Cl.
Bsn.
5
B♭ Tpt.
Hn.
Tbn.
5
Timp.
5
Vln I
pp
Vln II
pp
Vla
pp
Vlc
pp
Bass
pp

9
poco rall.
Sop
Alto
Ten
Bass
9
Fl.
dim.
Ob.
mf
poco rall.
p
B♭ Cl.
Bsn.
9
B♭ Tpt.
Hn.
Tbn.
9
Timp.
dim.
9
poco rall.
Vln I
dim.
pp
poco rall.
Vln II
dim.
pp
poco rall.
Vla
crescendo
pp
poco rall.
Vlc
mp
dim.
poco rall.
Bass
pp

13
same tempo
♩= 84
Sop
Alto
mp Meditatively and prayer-like
Ten
Do - - na no - bis re - - qui - em.
Bass
Fl.
Ob.
B♭ Cl.
Bsn.
B♭ Tpt.
Hn.
Tbn.
Timp.
pizz. (like harp)
Vln I
Vln II
Vla
Vlc
Bass

The Tenor text reads: Do - - na no - - bis no - bis re - qui -

21
Sop
Alto
Ten
em. Do - na no - bis re - qui - em et lux per -
Bass
Fl.
Ob.
B♭ Cl.
Bsn.
B♭ Tpt.
Hn.
Tbn.
Timp.
Vln I
Vln II
Vla
Vlc
Bass

25
Sop
Alto
Ten
pe - tu - a lu - - - ce - at
Bass
Fl.
dim.
Ob.
B♭ Cl.
Bsn.
B♭ Tpt.
Hn.
Tbn.
Timp.
Vln I
dim.
Vln II
dim.
Vla
dim.
Vlc
dim.
Bass

same tempo
♩= 88
29
Sop
Alto
Ten
Bass
Fl.
Ob.
Solo
mp
B♭ Cl.
legato
p
Bsn.
B♭ Tpt.
Hn.
Tbn.
Timp.
Vln I
arco
p
Vln II
Vla
Vlc
Bass

33
Sop
Alto
Ten
Bass
33
Fl.
Ob.
B♭ Cl.
Bsn.
33
B♭ Tpt.
Hn.
Tbn.
33
Timp.
33
Vln I
Vln II
Vla
Vlc
Bass

37
Sop
Alto
Ten
Bass
37
Fl.
Ob.
B♭ Cl.
Bsn.
37
B♭ Tpt.
Hn.
Tbn.
37
Timp.
37
Vln I
Vln II
Vla
Vlc
Bass

41
accel.
Sop
Alto
Ten
Bass
Fl.
Ob.
crescendo
B♭ Cl.
Bsn.
B♭ Tpt.
Hn.
Tbn.
Timp.
Vln I
Vln II
Vla
Vlc
Bass

Faster
♩= 96
45
Sop
Alto
Ten
Bass
Fl.
Ob.
B♭ Cl.
Bsn.
marcato
B♭ Tpt.
Hn.
Tbn.
Timp.
Vln I
Vln II
Vla
Vlc
Bass
f
mf

49
Sop
Alto
Ten
Bass
Fl.
Ob.
B♭ Cl.
Bsn.
B♭ Tpt.
Hn.
Tbn.
Timp.
Vln I
Vln II
Vla
Vlc
Bass

53
Sop
Alto
Ten
Bass
53
Fl.
Ob.
B♭ Cl.
Bsn.
53
B♭ Tpt.
Hn.
Tbn.
53
Timp.
53
Vln I
Vln II
Vla
Vlc
Bass

57
poco rall.
Sop
Alto
Ten
Bass
Fl.
Ob.
crescendo
B♭ Cl.
Bsn.
B♭ Tpt.
Hn.
Tbn.
Timp.
tr
crescendo
mp
Vln I
Vln II
Vla
Vlc
Bass

Faster
♩= 108
61
Sop
Alto
Ten
Bass
Solo marcato
Fl.
Ob.
B♭ Cl.
Bsn.
B♭ Tpt.
Hn.
Tbn.
Timp.
Vln I
Vln II
Vla
Vlc
Bass
(drop back)
(drop back)
(drop back)

65
Sop
Alto
Ten
Bass
65
Fl.
crescendo
Ob.
crescendo
B♭ Cl.
(drop back)
Bsn.
(drop back)
65
B♭ Tpt.
Hn.
(drop back)
Tbn.
(drop back)
65
Timp.
tr
65
Vln I
Vln II
Vla
Vlc
Bass

69
rit.
Sop
Alto
Ten
Bass
crescendo rit.
Fl.
Ob.
B♭ Cl.
Bsn.
B♭ Tpt.
Hn.
Tbn.
Timp.
Vln I
Vln II
Vla
Vlc
Bass
crescendo
ff
(drop back)
3

Andante
♩= 88
73
Sop
Alto
Ten
Bass
mp
Do - na no - bis Do - na no - bis Do - na no - bis re - qui -
Fl.
Ob.
B♭ Cl.
Bsn.
B♭ Tpt.
Hn.
p
Tbn.
Timp.
legato
Vln I
Vln II
Vla
Vlc
Bass
p

77
Sop
Alto
Ten
Bass
mp
Do - na no - bis Do - na no - bis Do - na no - bis re - qui -
em. Do - na no - bis Do - na no -
Fl.
Ob.
p
B♭ Cl.
Bsn.
B♭ Tpt.
Hn.
Tbn.
Timp.
Vln I
Vln II
Vla
Vlc
Bass

81
Sop
Alto
em. Do - na no - bis re - - - qui - em.
Ten
mp
Do - na no - bis Do - na no - bis
Bass
bis Do - na no - bis re - - - qui - em.
81
Fl.
Ob.
B♭ Cl.
p
Bsn.
81
B♭ Tpt.
Hn.
Tbn.
81
Timp.
81
Vln I
Vln II
Vla
Vlc
Bass

85
Sop
Alto
Ten
Bass
Fl.
Ob.
B♭ Cl.
Bsn.
B♭ Tpt.
Hn.
Tbn.
Timp.
Vln I
Vln II
Vla
Vlc
Bass
mp
Do - na no - bis Do - na
Do - na no - bis re - qui - em. Do - na no - bis Do -
Do - na no - bis re - qui - em. Do - na no - - bis
Do - na no - bis re - qui - em. Do - - na
p
pp
dim.

89
Sop
no - bis Do - na no - bis re - qui - em. Do - na
Alto
na no - bis re - qui - em. Do - na
Ten
re - - - - qui - - - em. Do - na
Bass
no - - - bis re - - - qui - em. Do - na
Fl.
Ob.
B♭ Cl.
Bsn.
B♭ Tpt.
Hn.
Tbn.
Timp.
Vln I
Vln II
Vla
Vlc
Bass

93
Sop
Alto
Ten
Bass
no - bis re - - - qui - em.
no - bis re - - - qui - em.
no - bis re - qui-em. Do - na no - bis Do - na no - bis
no - bis re - qui-em. Do - na no - bis Do - na no - bis
decrescendo
Fl.
Ob.
B♭ Cl.
Bsn.
B♭ Tpt.
Hn.
Tbn.
Timp.
Vln I
Vln II
Vla
Vlc
Bass
legato

97
Sop
Alto
Ten
Bass
Fl.
Ob.
B♭ Cl.
Bsn.
B♭ Tpt.
Hn.
Tbn.
Timp.
Vln I
Vln II
Vla
Vlc
Bass
Do - na no - bis Do - na
Do - na no - bis Do - na
Do - na no - bis re - qui - em. Do - na
Do - na no - bis re - qui - em. Do - na
mp
p

101
Sop
Alto
Ten
Bass
crescendo
no - bis Do - na no - bis re - qui - em. Do - na no - - bis
no - bis Do - na no - bis re - qui - em. Do - na no - - bis
no - - - - bis re - qui - em.
no - - - - bis re - qui - em.
Fl.
Ob.
B♭ Cl.
Bsn.
B♭ Tpt.
Hn.
Tbn.
Timp.
Vln I
Vln II
Vla
Vlc
Bass

105
Sop
Alto
Ten
Bass
Fl.
Ob.
B♭ Cl.
Bsn.
B♭ Tpt.
Hn.
Tbn.
Timp.
Vln I
Vln II
Vla
Vlc
Bass
mf
mp
crescendo
re - - - qui - em. Do - na no - bis
re - - - qui - em. Do - na no - - -
Do - na no - bis Do - na no - bis Do - na no - bis re - qui -
Do - na no - bis Do - na no - bis Do - na no - bis re - qui -

109
crescendo
Sop
re - - qui - em. Do - - - - - - na
Alto
bis Do - na no - bis Do - na no - bis Do - na no - bis
Ten
em. Do - - - na no - - - bis Do - na
Bass
em. Do - na no - bis Do - na no - - - bis Do - na
Fl.
Ob.
B♭ Cl.
Bsn.
B♭ Tpt.
Hn.
Tbn.
Timp.
Vln I
Vln II
Vla
Vlc
Bass

113
Sop
Alto
Ten
Bass
crescendo
rit.
ff
Do-na no - - - bis re - qui - em.
no - - - - bis re - qui - em.
Fl.
Ob.
B♭ Cl.
Bsn.
B♭ Tpt.
Hn.
Tbn.
Timp.
Vln I
Vln II
Vla
Vlc
Bass
tr
f

Andante
♩= 88
117
Sop
Alto
Ten
Bass
Fl.
Solo
Ob.
mp
B♭ Cl.
Bsn.
B♭ Tpt.
legato
Hn.
Tbn.
Timp.
Vln I
Vln II
Vla
Vlc
Bass
dim.
p

37

125
accel.
Sop
Alto
Ten
Bass
Fl.
Ob.
B♭ Cl.
Bsn.
B♭ Tpt.
Hn.
Tbn.
Timp.
Vln I
Vln II
Vla
Vlc
Bass
p
pp
mp
decrescendo

Faster
♩= 92
129
Sop
Alto
Ten
Bass
Fl.
Solo
mp
Ob.
B♭ Cl.
p
Bsn.
B♭ Tpt.
legato
crescendo
(drop back)
Hn.
Tbn.
Timp.
Vln I
Vln II
Vla
Vlc
Bass

133
Sop
Alto
Ten
Bass
133
Fl.
Ob.
B♭ Cl.
Bsn.
133
B♭ Tpt.
Hn.
Tbn.
133
Timp.
133
Vln I
Vln II
Vla
Vlc
Bass
crescendo
(drop back)
crescendo
(drop back)
crescendo
crescendo

41

Faster
♩ = 100
141
Sop
Do - na no - bis re - qui - em.
Alto
Do - na no - bis re - qui - em.
Ten
Do - na no - bis re - qui - em.
Bass
Do - na no - bis re - qui - em.
Fl.
Ob.
B♭ Cl.
Bsn.
B♭ Tpt.
Hn.
Tbn.
Timp.
Vln I
Vln II
Vla
Vlc
Bass
f
mf

145
Sop
Do - na no - bis no - bis re - qui -
Alto
Do - na no - bis no - bis re - qui -
Ten
Do - na no - bis no - bis re - qui -
Bass
Do - na no - bis no - bis re - qui -
145
Fl.
Ob.
B♭ Cl.
Bsn.
145
B♭ Tpt.
Hn.
Tbn.
145
Timp.
145
Vln I
Vln II
Vla
Vlc
Bass

149
Sop
em. Do - na no - bis re - qui - em et lux per -
Alto
em. Do - na no - bis re - qui - em et lux per -
Ten
em. Do - na no - bis re - qui - em et lux per -
Bass
em. Do - na no - bis re - qui - em et lux per -
149
Fl.
Ob.
B♭ Cl.
Bsn.
149
B♭ Tpt.
Hn.
Tbn.
149
Timp.
149
Vln I
Vln II
Vla
Vlc
Bass

153
rit.
Sop
pe - tu - a lu - - - ce - at
Alto
pe - tu - a lu - - - ce - at
Ten
pe - tu - a lu - - - ce - at
Bass
pe - tu - a lu - - - ce - at
Fl.
Ob.
B♭ Cl.
Bsn.
B♭ Tpt.
Hn.
Tbn.
Timp.
Vln I
Vln II
Vla
Vlc
Bass

Slower
♩= 92
157
Sop
Alto
Ten
Bass
Fl.
Ob.
B♭ Cl.
Bsn.
B♭ Tpt.
Solo legato
mp
Hn.
Tbn.
Timp.
Vln I
Vln II
Vla
Vlc
Bass
p

161
Sop
Alto
Ten
Bass
161
Fl.
Ob.
B♭ Cl.
Bsn.
161
B♭ Tpt.
Hn.
Tbn.
161
Timp.
161
Vln I
Vln II
Vla
Vlc
Bass

165
Sop
Alto
Ten
Bass
165
Fl.
Ob.
B♭ Cl.
Bsn.
165
B♭ Tpt.
Hn.
Tbn.
165
Timp.
165
Vln I
Vln II
Vla
Vlc
mp
Bass

169
rit.
Sop
Alto
Ten
Bass
Fl.
Ob.
B♭ Cl.
Bsn.
B♭ Tpt.
Hn.
Tbn.
Timp.
Vln I
Vln II
Vla
Vlc
Bass
mp

Slower
♩= 80
173
Sop
Alto
Ten
Bass
Fl.
Solo
Ob.
B♭ Cl.
Bsn.
B♭ Tpt.
Hn.
Tbn.
Timp.
Vln I
Vln II
Vla
Vlc
Bass
p
pp

177
Sop
Alto
Ten
Bass
rit.
Fl.
Ob.
B♭ Cl.
Bsn.
B♭ Tpt.
Hn.
Tbn.
Timp.
tr
Vln I
Vln II
Vla
Vlc
Bass
ppp

II. Eleison

Requiem II: Eleison

54

9
Sop
Alt
Ten
Bass
9
Fl.
Ob.
B♭ Cl.
Bsn.
9
B♭ Tpt.
Hn.
Tbn.
9
Timp.
9
Vln I
Vln II
Vla
Vlc
Bass
dim.
rit.

13
Sop
Alt
Ten
Bass
13
Fl.
Ob.
B♭ Cl.
Bsn.
13
B♭ Tpt.
Hn.
Tbn.
13
Timp.
13
Vln I
Vln II
Vla
Vlc
Bass
ten.
ten.
ten.
ten.
ten.

17
rit.
Moderato
♩ = 108
joyfully
mf
Sop
In hea - - - ven and on
Alt
In hea - - - ven and on
Ten
In hea - - - ven and on
Bass
In hea - - - ven and on
Fl.
Ob.
B♭ Cl.
Bsn.
B♭ Tpt.
Hn.
Tbn.
Timp.
Vln I
Vln II
Vla
Vlc
Bass
mp

21
Sop
earth,
by
day
and
Alt
earth,
by
day
and
Ten
earth,
by
day
and
Bass
earth,
by
day
and
21
Fl.
Ob.
B♭ Cl.
Bsn.
21
B♭ Tpt.
Hn.
Tbn.
21
Timp.
21
Vln I
Vln II
Vla
Vlc
Bass

25
Sop
night
on
high
seas,
high
Alt
night
on
high
seas,
high
Ten
night
on
high
seas,
high
Bass
night
on
high
seas,
high
Fl.
Ob.
B♭ Cl.
Bsn.
B♭ Tpt.
Hn.
Tbn.
Timp.
Vln I
Vln II
Vla
Vlc
Bass

29
Sop
seas, on high seas and in
Alt
seas, on high seas and in
Ten
seas, on high seas and in
Bass
seas, on high seas and in
29
Fl.
Ob.
B♭ Cl.
Bsn.
29
B♭ Tpt.
Hn.
Tbn.
29
Timp.
29
Vln I
Vln II
Vla
Vlc
Bass

33
Sop
deep
dales,
Alt
deep
dales,
Ten
deep
dales,
Bass
deep
dales,
Fl.
crescendo
(bring out 8th notes)
mp
Ob.
crescendo
mp
B♭ Cl.
crescendo
mp
Bsn.
crescendo
mp
B♭ Tpt.
Hn.
Tbn.
Timp.
Vln I
decrescendo
Vln II
decrescendo
Vla
decrescendo
Vlc
decrescendo
Bass

Faster ♩ = 112
37
Sop
un - der trees and in the o - pen, un - der trees
Alt
un - der trees and in the o - pen un - der un - der trees
Ten
un - der trees and in the o - pen un - der un - der trees
Bass
un - der trees and in the o - pen, un - der trees un - der
Fl.
Ob.
B♭ Cl.
Bsn.
B♭ Tpt.
Hn.
Tbn.
Timp.
Vln I
Vln II
Vla
Vlc
Bass

41
crescendo
Sop
and in the o - pen, in gla - ring sun
Alt
and in the o - pen, in gla - ring sun
Ten
and in the o - pen, in gla - ring sun
Bass
trees and in the o - pen, in gla - ring sun
Fl.
Ob.
B♭ Cl.
Bsn.
B♭ Tpt.
Hn.
Tbn
Timp.
Vln I
Vln II
Vla
Vlc
Bass

45
Sop
gla - - - ring sun and un-der a si - - - lent
Alt
gla - - - ring sun un-der a si - - - lent
Ten
gla - - - ring sun and un-der a si - - - lent
Bass
gla - ring sun and un-der a si - - - lent
decrescendo
mp
Fl.
Ob.
B♭ Cl.
Bsn.
ppp
Tpt.
Hn.
Tbn.
Timp.
Vln I
Vln II
Vla
Vlc
Bass

49
Sop
moon, un - der a si - - - - - - lent
Alt
moon, un - der a si - - - - - - lent
Ten
moon, un - der a si - - - - - - lent
Bass
moon, un - der a si - - - - - - lent
Fl.
Ob.
B♭ Cl.
Bsn.
B♭ Tpt.
Hn.
Tbn.
Timp.
Vln I
Vln II
Vla
Vlc
Bass

53
Sop
mp crescendo f
moon, with ev' - ry bird
Alt
mp crescendo f
moon, with ev' - ry bird
Ten
mp crescendo f
moon, with ev' - ry bird
Bass
mp crescendo f
moon, with ev' - ry bird
Fl.
p crescendo mf
Ob.
p crescendo mf
B♭ Cl.
p crescendo mf
Bsn.
p crescendo mf
B♭ Tpt.
Hn.
Tbn.
Timp.
Vln I
crescendo
Vln II
mf
Vla
mf
Vlc
mf
Bass
mf

57
Sop
with ev' - ry bird
with ev' - ry
Alt
with ev' - ry bird
with ev' - ry
Ten
with ev' - ry bird
with ev' - ry
Bass
with ev' - ry bird ev' - ry bird
with ev' - ry
Fl.
Ob.
B♭ Cl.
Bsn.
B♭ Tpt.
Hn.
Tbn.
Timp.
Vln I
Vln II
Vla
Vlc
Bass

61
Sop
bird and fish, with all a - ni-mals, with all
Alt
bird and fish, with all a - ni-mals, with all
Ten
bird and fish, with all a - ni-mals, with all
Bass
bird and fish, with all
Fl.
Ob.
B♭ Cl.
Bsn.
B♭ Tpt.
Hn.
Tbn.
Timp.
Vln I
Vln II
Vla
Vlc
Bass

Sop: a - - - ni - mals, both tamed and

Alt: a - - - ni - mals, both tamed and

Ten: a - - - ni - mals, both tamed tamed and

Bass: a - - - ni - mals, both tamed tamed and

69
accel.
Sop
wild, and wild,
Alt
wild, and wild,
Ten
wild, and wild,
Bass
wild, and wild,
Fl.
Ob.
B♭ Cl.
Bsn.
B♭ Tpt.
Hn.
Tbn.
Timp.
Vln I
Vln II
Vla
Vlc
Bass
accel.
dim.

73
Faster
♩= 116
mf
Sop
we will re -
Alt
Ten
Bass
Fl.
dim.
Ob.
mp
B♭ Cl.
Bsn.
B♭ Tpt.
Hn.
Tbn.
Timp.
Vln I
p
Vln II
Vla
Vlc
Bass

joice re - joice with those who re - joice

81
Sop
Alt
Ten
Bass
who re - joice
mf
we will re -
Fl.
Ob.
B♭ Cl.
Bsn.
mp
B♭ Tpt.
Hn.
mp
Tbn.
Timp.
Vln I
Vln II
Vla
Vlc
Bass

85
Sop
Alt
Ten
joice re - joice with those who re - joice
Bass
85
Fl.
Ob.
B♭ Cl.
Bsn.
85
B♭ Tpt.
Hn.
Tbn.
85
Timp.
85
Vln I
Vln II
Vla
Vlc
Bass

89
Sop
Alt
Ten
Bass
mf
we will re -
who re - joice
Fl.
Ob.
B♭ Cl.
Bsn.
mf
B♭ Tpt.
Hn.
Tbn.
mp
Timp.
Vln I
Vln II
Vla
Vlc
Bass

93
Sop
Alt
joice re - joice with those who re - joice
Ten
Bass
93
Fl.
Ob.
B♭ Cl.
Bsn.
93
B♭ Tpt.
Hn.
Tbn.
93
Timp.
93
Vln I
Vln II
Vla
Vlc
Bass

97
Sop
Alt
who re - joice
Ten
mf
Bass
we will re -
Fl.
Ob.
B♭ Cl.
Bsn.
B♭ Tpt.
Hn.
Tbn.
mp
Timp.
Vln I
Vln II
Vla
Vlc
Bass

joice   re - joice   with   those   who   re - joice

78

105
accel.
Allegro
♩= 120
Sop
Alt
Ten
Bass
who re - joice
we will re -
Fl.
Ob.
B♭ Cl.
Bsn.
crescendo
B♭ Tpt.
Hn.
Tbn.
Timp.
Vln I
Vln II
Vla
Vlc
Bass
triplets marcato

joice re - joice with those who re - joice

joice re - joice with those who re - joice

joice re - joice with those who re - joice

joice re - joice with those who re - joice

113
Sop
who re - joice
Alt
re - joice we will re - joice re - joice with
Ten
who re - joice we will re - joice re -
Bass
who re - joice we will re -
Fl.
Ob.
B♭ Cl.
Bsn.
B♭ Tpt.
Hn.
Tbn.
Timp.
Vln I
Vln II
Vla
Vlc
Bass

117
Sop
we will re - joice re - joice with those who re -
Alt
those who re - joice with those who re -
Ten
joice with those who re - joice with those who re -
Bass
joice re - joice with those who re - joice
Fl.
Ob.
B♭ Cl.
Bsn.
B♭ Tpt.
Hn.
Tbn.
Timp.
Vln I
Vln II
Vla
Vlc
Bass

121
rit.
Moderato
♩= 100
Sop
Alt
Ten
Bass
joice
joice
joice
who re - joice
and
and
and
and
Fl.
Ob.
B♭ Cl.
Bsn.
B♭ Tpt.
Hn.
Tbn.
Timp.
Vln I
Vln II
Vla
Vlc
Bass
p
pp

125
Sop
weep
weep
(♮)
with
Alt
weep
weep
with
Ten
weep
weep
with
Bass
weep
and
weep
with
125
Fl.
Ob.
B♭ Cl.
Bsn.
125
B♭ Tpt.
Hn.
Tbn.
125
Timp.
125
Vln I
Vln II
(♮)
Vla
(♮)
Vlc
Bass

129
Sop
those
who
weep.
Alt
those
who
weep.
Ten
those
who
weep.
Bass
those
who
weep.
129
Fl.
Ob.
B♭ Cl.
Bsn.
129
B♭ Tpt.
Hn.
Tbn.
129
Timp.
129
Vln I
Vln II
Vla
Vlc
Bass

Requiem II: Eleison

137
Sop
Alt
Ten
Bass
137
Fl.
Ob.
B♭ Cl.
Bsn.
137
B♭ Tpt.
Hn.
Tbn.
137
Timp.
137
Vln I
Vln II
Vla
Vlc
Bass
3

Requiem II: Eleison

145
Sop
Alt
Ten
Bass
145
Fl.
Ob.
B♭ Cl.
Bsn.
145
B♭ Tpt.
Hn.
Tbn.
145
Timp.
145
Vln I
Vln II
Vla
Vlc
Bass
ten.
ten.
ten.
ten.
ten.

Requiem II: Eleison

153
Sop
Alt
We will weep
Ten
mp
We will weep
Bass
153
Fl.
Ob.
p
B♭ Cl.
p
Bsn.
153
B♭ Tpt.
Hn.
Tbn.
153
Timp.
153
Vln I
Vln II
Vla
Vlc
Bass

157
Sop
Alt
Ten
mp
We will weep
Bass
We will weep
We will
157
Fl.
Ob.
B♭ Cl.
Bsn.
p
157
B♭ Tpt.
Hn.
Tbn.
157
Timp.
157
Vln I
Vln II
Vla
Vlc
Bass

161
Sop
mp
We will weep
Alt
mp
We will weep
Ten
We will weep
Bass
weep
161
Fl.
Ob.
B♭ Cl.
Bsn.
161
B♭ Tpt.
Hn.
Tbn.
161
Timp.
161
Vln I
Vln II
Vla
Vlc
Bass

Requiem II: Eleison

169
Sop
weep with those who
Alt
weep with those who
Ten
weep with those who
Bass
weep with those who
Fl.
Ob.
B♭ Cl.
Bsn.
B♭ Tpt.
Hn.
Tbn.
Timp.
Vln I
Vln II
Vla
Vlc
Bass

173
Sop
Alt
Ten
Bass
decrescendo
weep
We will
We will weep
Fl.
Ob.
B♭ Cl.
Bsn.
B♭ Tpt.
Hn.
Tbn.
Timp.
Vln I
Vln II
Vla
Vlc
Bass

177
Sop
Alt
Ten
Bass
We will
We will weep
weep
Fl.
Ob.
B♭ Cl.
Bsn.
B♭ Tpt.
Hn.
Tbn.
Timp.
Vln I
Vln II
Vla
Vlc
Bass

181
Sop
weep
mp
We
Alt
We
will
weep
mp
Ten
We
will
Bass
181
Fl.
Ob.
B♭ Cl.
Bsn.
181
B♭ Tpt.
p
Hn.
p
Tbn.
181
Timp.
181
crescendo
Vln I
mp
Vln II
mp
Vla
mp
Vlc
mp
Bass

185
Sop
Alt
Ten
Bass
will
weep
We will
We
will
weep
We will
weep
weep
We will weep
crescendo
Fl.
Ob.
B♭ Cl.
Bsn.
B♭ Tpt.
Hn.
Tbn.
Timp.
Vln I
Vln II
Vla
Vlc
Bass
p
3

189
Sop
weep
We will weep
Alt
weep
We will weep
Ten
We will weep
Bass
We will weep
Fl.
Ob.
B♭ Cl.
Bsn.
B♭ Tpt.
Hn.
Tbn.
Timp.
Vln I
Vln II
Vla
Vlc
Bass

193
Sop
Alt
Ten
Bass
decrescendo
p
We will weep
We will
Fl.
Ob.
B♭ Cl.
Bsn.
B♭ Tpt.
Hn.
Tbn.
Timp.
Vln I
Vln II
Vla
Vlc
Bass
mf
pp
bring out oving notes

197
Sop
weep
Alt
We will weep
Ten
We will
Bass
Fl.
Ob.
B♭ Cl.
Bsn.
B♭ Tpt.
Hn.
Tbn.
Timp.
Vln I
Vln II
Vla
Vlc
Bass

201
Sop
weep
We will
Alt
weep
Ten
weep
We will
Bass
We will weep
Fl.
Ob.
B♭ Cl.
Bsn.
B♭ Tpt.
Hn.
Tbn.
Timp.
Vln I
Vln II
Vla
Vlc
Bass

205
Sop
Alt
Ten
Bass
crescendo
weep
We
will
weep
We
will
weep
weep
We
will
weep
We
will
weep
Fl.
Ob.
B♭ Cl.
Bsn.
B♭ Tpt.
Hn.
Tbn.
Timp.
Vln I
Vln II
Vla
Vlc
Bass
p
tr
3

209
rit.
Sop
with those who weep
Alt
with those who weep
Ten
with those who weep
Bass
with those who weep
Fl.
Ob.
B♭ Cl.
Bsn.
B♭ Tpt.
Hn.
Tbn.
Timp.
Vln I
Vln II
Vla
Vlc
Bass
3

Andante
♩= 88
213
mp
E - - - - - le - - i - son,
Sop
Alt
Ten
Bass
Fl.
Ob.
B♭ Cl.
Bsn.
p
E - - - - - le - - - i - - - - - -
B♭ Tpt.
Hn.
Tbn.
Timp.
Vln I
Vln II
Vla
Vlc
Bass
f
p

217
Sop
Alt
Ten
Bass
mf
e - - - - - - - - - - -
Fl.
Ob.
B♭ Cl.
Bsn.
decrescendo
B♭ Tpt.
Hn.
Tbn.
Timp.
Vln I
Vln II
Vla
Vlc
Bass
crescendo
p

221
Sop
le - - i - son, e -
Alt
le - - i - son, e -
Ten
le - - i - son, e -
Bass
le - - i - son, e -
Fl.
Ob.
B♭ Cl.
Bsn.
decrescendo
B♭ Tpt.
Hn.
Tbn.
Timp.
Vln I
Vln II
Vla
Vlc
Bass
mf
p

225
Sop
le - - - i - son.
Alt
le - - - i - son.
Ten
le - - - i - son.
Bass
le - - - i - son.
Fl.
Ob.
B♭ Cl.
Bsn.
B♭ Tpt.
Hn.
Tbn.
Timp.
Vln I
Vln II
Vla
Vlc
Bass

a tempo
♩= 88
229
rit.
Sop
Alt
Ten
Bass
Fl.
Ob.
B♭ Cl.
Bsn.
B♭ Tpt.
Hn.
Tbn.
Timp.
Vln I
Vln II
Vla
Solo
Vlc
Bass

233
Sop
Alt
Ten
Bass
rit.
Fl.
Ob.
B♭ Cl.
Bsn.
decrescendo
p
B♭ Tpt.
Hn.
Tbn.
pp
Timp.
tr
Vln I
Vln II
Vla
Vlc
Bass

III. Dies Irae

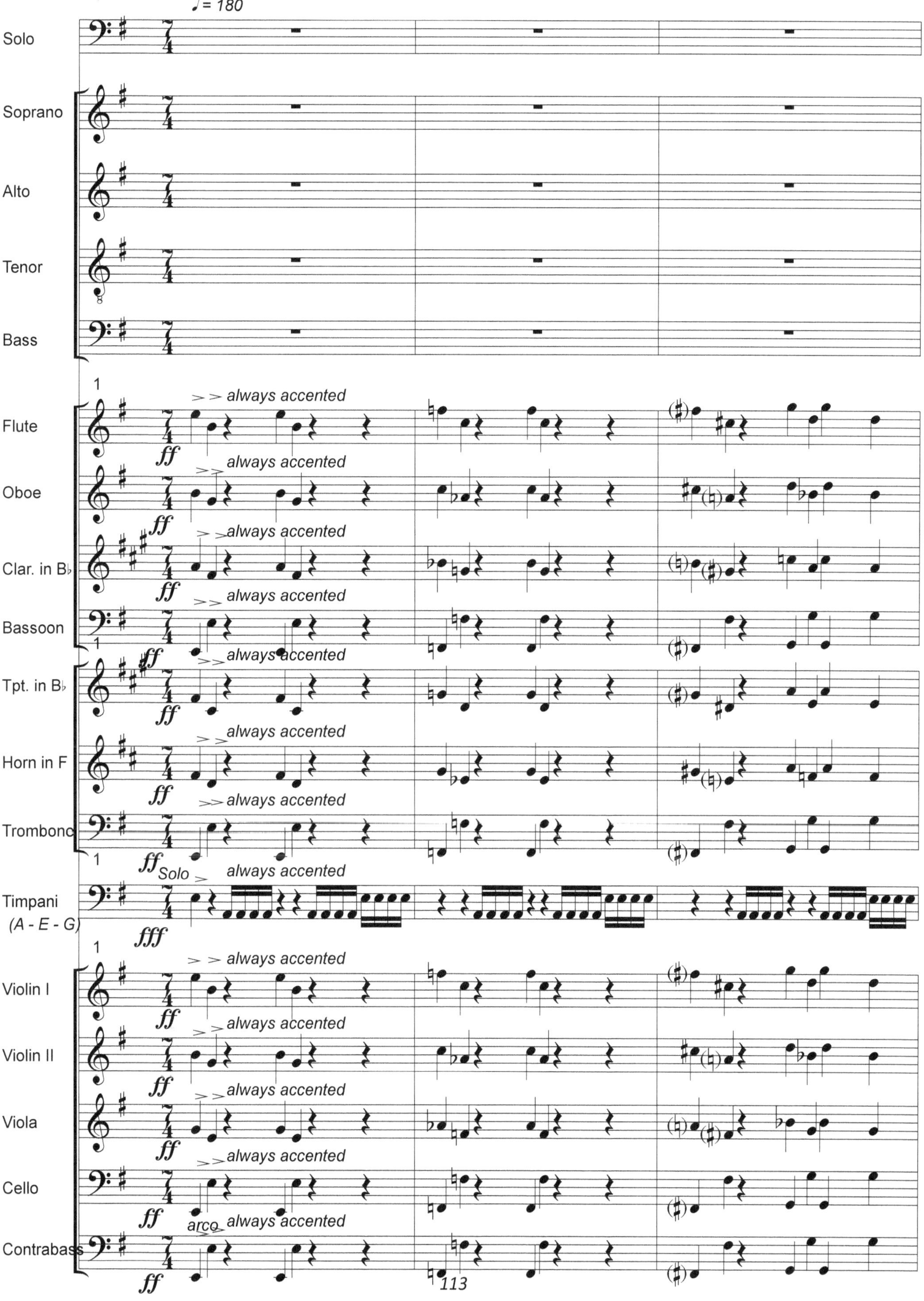

4
Solo
Sop
Alto
Ten
Bass
Fl.
Ob.
B♭ Cl.
Bsn.
B♭ Tpt.
Hn.
Tbn.
Timp.
Vln I
Vln II
Vla
Vlc
Bass

7
♩= 88 Andante
Solo
Sop
Alto
Ten
Bass
ff We weep mp We
Fl.
Ob.
B♭ Cl.
Bsn.
B♭ Tpt.
Hn.
Tbn.
Timp.
tr
Vln I
Vln II
Vla
Vlc
Bass
p

10
Solo
Sop
weep for the death that is in store for
Alto
weep for the death that is in store for
Ten
weep for the death that is in store for
Bass
weep for the death that is in store for
Fl.
Ob.
B♭ Cl.
Bsn.
B♭ Tpt.
Hn.
Tbn.
Timp.
Vln I
Vln II
Vla
Vlc
Bass

14
Solo
Sop
all of us and for the
Alto
all of us all of us and for the
Ten
all of us all of us and for the
Bass
all of us and for the
Fl.
Ob.
B♭ Cl.
Bsn.
B♭ Tpt.
Hn.
Tbn.
Timp.
Vln I
Vln II
Vla
Vlc
Bass

18

Solo

Sop

Alto

deaths   we   have   lived   to   see

Ten

deaths   we   have   lived   to   see

Bass

deaths   we   have   lived   to   see

18   deaths   we   have   lived   to   see

Fl.

Ob.

B♭ Cl.

Bsn.

18

B♭ Tpt.

Hn.

Tbn.

18

Timp.

18

Vln I

Vln II

Vla

Vlc

Bass

22
Solo
Sop
to see in the pass - ing of our
Alto
to see in the pass - ing of our
Ten
to see in the pass - ing of our
Bass
to see in the pass - ing of our
Fl.
Ob.
B♭ Cl.
Bsn.
B♭ Tpt.
Hn.
Tbn.
Timp.
Vln I
Vln II
Vla
Vlc
Bass

26
Solo
Sop
friends and kin, our bro - thers and sis - ters, our
Alto
friends and kin, our bro - thers and sis - ters, our
Ten
friends and kin, our bro - thers and sis - ters, our
Bass
friends and kin, our bro - thers and sis - ters, our
Fl.
Ob.
B♭ Cl.
Bsn.
B♭ Tpt.
Hn.
Tbn.
Timp.
Vln I
Vln II
Vla
Vlc
Bass

30
Solo
Sop
pa - rents and chil - dren - - - the mor - ta - li - ty of our
Alto
pa - rents and chil - dren - - - the mor - ta - li - ty of our
Ten
pa - rents and chil - dren - - - the mor - ta - li - ty of our
Bass
pa - rents and chil - dren - - - the mor - ta - li - ty of our
Fl.
Ob.
B♭ Cl.
Bsn.
B♭ Tpt.
Hn.
Tbn.
Timp.
Vln I
Vln II
Vla
Vlc
Bass

34
Solo
Sop
chil - - - dren most of all fills us with
Alto
chil - - - dren most of all fills us with
Ten
chil - - - dren most of all fills us with
Bass
chil - - - dren most of all fills us with
Fl.
Ob.
B♭ Cl.
Bsn.
B♭ Tpt.
Hn.
Tbn.
Timp.
Vln I
Vln II
Vla
Vlc
Bass

38
♩= 84 Slower
Solo
Sop
Alto
Ten
Bass
decrescendo
pp
dead - ly fear.
Sa - - - -
Fl.
Ob.
B♭ Cl.
Bsn.
B♭ Tpt.
Hn.
Tbn
Timp.
ppp
tr
Vln I
Vln II
Vla
Vlc
Bass

42
Solo
Sop
le no - - - bis, fons pi - e -
Alto
le no - - - bis, fons pi - e -
Ten
le no - - - bis, fons pi - e -
Bass
le no - - - bis, fons pi - e -
42
Fl.
Ob.
B♭ Cl.
Bsn.
42
B♭ Tpt.
Hn.
Tbn.
42
Timp.
42
Vln I
Vln II
Vla
Vlc
Bass

125

49
♩= 88 Andante
Solo
Sop
mf
We weep o - ver the tra - gic deaths in
Alto
mf
We weep o - ver the tra - gic deaths in
Ten
mf
We weep o - ver the tra - gic deaths in
Bass
mf
We weep o - ver the tra - gic deaths in
Fl.
Ob.
B♭ Cl.
Bsn.
B♭ Tpt.
Hn.
Tbn.
Timp.
Vln I
mp
Vln II
Vla
Vlc
mf
Bass

53
Solo
Sop
na - tu - ral dis - as - - - ters and
Alto
na - tu - ral dis - as - - - ters and
Ten
na - tu - ral dis - as - - - ters and
Bass
na - tu - ral dis - as - - - ters and
Fl.
Ob.
B♭ Cl.
Bsn.
B♭ Tpt.
Hn.
Tbn.
Timp.
Vln I
Vln II
Vla
Vlc
Bass

o - ver the shame - ful deaths of our dis -

o - ver the shame - ful deaths of our dis -

o - ver the shame - ful deaths of our dis -

o - ver the shame - ful deaths of our dis -

61
Solo
Sop
as - trous hu - - - - - man his - to - ry,
Alto
as - trous hu - - - - - man his - to - ry,
Ten
as - trous hu - - - - - man his - to - ry,
Bass
as - trous hu - - - - - man his - to - ry,
Fl.
Ob.
B♭ Cl.
Bsn.
B♭ Tpt.
Hn.
Tbn.
Timp.
Vln I
Vln II
Vla
Vlc
Bass

Sop: in which to this day a - gain and a - gain

Ten: in which to this day a - gain and a - gain

Bass: in which to this day a - gain and a - gain

69
rit.
Agitato
♩= 180
Solo
Sop
lives are en - ded be - fore their time.
Alto
lives are en - ded be - fore their time.
Ten
lives are en - ded be - fore their time.
Bass
lives are en - ded be - fore their
Fl.
Ob.
B♭ Cl.
Bsn.
B♭ Tpt.
Hn.
Tbn.
Timp.
fff
Vln I
Vln II
Vla
Vlc
Bass

73
Solo
Sop
Alto
Ten
Bass
ff
always accented
Di-es i-rae, di-es il-la. sol-vet sae-clum
Fl.
Ob.
B♭ Cl.
Bsn.
B♭ Tpt.
Hn.
Tbn.
Timp.
(A - E - G)
Vln I
Vln II
Vla
Vlc
Bass

Men, women and children are killed   for the co-lor of their

in fa - vil-la.

in fa - vil-la.

in fa - vil-la.

in fa - vil-la.

skin,   for their gen-der   for their faith-ven for their faith in a just   and rea-son-a-ble world - - - for their o - ri - gin for their po - ver - ty - which

135

by it-self is dead - ly.

They pe - ish, They pe - rish locked in

137

pri-sons and work-ing plants-posed on o-pen seas and in tor - rid de-serts slaugh - tered   in   e - ter - nal   wars   ripped a - part   by ro-bot de-vi-ces   ex-iled in un-known lands which   do not wel-come them or tied to a

100
rit.
Agitato
♩= 180
Solo
place, that can - not give them life..
Sop
Alto
Ten
Bass
Fl.
Ob.
B♭ Cl.
Bsn.
B♭ Tpt.
Hn.
Tbn.
Timp.
tr
Vln I
Vln II
Vla
Vlc
Bass
always accented
ff
arco

142

To this day time and a-

109
crescendo
Solo
gain and in all pla - ces there are ma - ster ra - ces, who
Sop
Alto
Ten
Bass
109
(continue)
crescendo
Fl.
(continue)
crescendo
Ob.
(continue)
crescendo
B♭ Cl.
(continue)
crescendo
Bsn.
109
B♭ Tpt.
Hn.
(continue)
crescendo
Tbn.
109
tr
tr
crescendo
tr
Timp.
109
Vln I
Vln II
Vla
Vlc
crescendo
Bass

ar-ro-gate the right   to   rule o-ver life and death of   o-ther hu - man be-ings in that short time be-fore their own de-mise. And as a hu-man spe-cies we subdue   the whole   earth.   We sub - due   the whole

121
Solo
mp
earth.
We set the odds
for the
Sop
Alto
Ten
Bass
121
Fl.
subito f
p
ten.
(continue)
Ob.
subito f
p
ten.
(continue)
B♭ Cl.
subito f
p
ten.
(continue)
Bsn.
subito f
p
ten.
(continue)
121
B♭ Tpt.
Hn.
Tbn.
ff
subito p
ten.
(continue)
121
Timp.
tr
p
121
Vln I
Vln II
Vla
Vlc
Bass
subito f
p

but - ter-fly   to sur - vive   in the ge - ne-ti cal-ly al-tered mo-no-cul-ture.

We de-cide   which plants and a - ni-mals must die   be-fore their

151

Solo

Sop

sol - vet   sae-clum   in   fa - vil - la.

Alto

sol - vet   sae - clum   in   fa - vil - la.

Ten

sol-vet   sae - clum   in   fa - vil - la.

Bass

sol - vet   sae - clum   in   fa - vil - la.

Fl.

Ob.

B♭ Cl.

Bsn.

B♭ Tpt.

Hn.

Tbn.

Timp.

Vln I

Vln II

Vla

Vlc

Bass

135
Andante
mp
♩= 84
crescendo
rit.
Solo
Do - num fac re-mis-si - o - nis an-te di-em ra-ti - o-nis.
Sop
pp
Alto
pp
Ten
pp
Bass
pp
Fl.
Ob.
B♭ Cl.
ppp
Bsn.
ppp
B♭ Tpt.
ppp
Hn.
ppp
Tbn.
pp
Timp.
ppp
Vln I
pp
Vln II
pp
Vla
pp
Vlc
pp
Bass
pp

We de-stroy the world   be-cause that is ea-si-er   and more con-ve nient than to save   the world   time   and a-gain

Solo: time and a-gain time and a-gain time and a-

148
Solo
mp
gain and in all pla - ces. And then we be -
Sop
Alto
Ten
Bass
148
Fl.
p
Ob.
p
B♭ Cl.
p
Bsn.
p
148
B♭ Tpt.
p
Hn.
p
Tbn.
148
tr
Timp.
tr
p
tr
148
Vln I
Vln II
Vla
Vlc
Bass
p

151
Solo
weep be - weep
dwindling gla-ciers bloa-ted de-serts
Sop
Alto
Ten
Bass
Fl.
Ob.
p
B♭ Cl.
Bsn.
B♭ Tpt.
Hn.
Tbn.
Timp.
tr
Vln I
Vln II
Vla
Vlc
Bass

e-ro-ded hills   cut-down fo - rests   pol-lu-ted wa-ters

159

Agitato
♩= 180
157
Solo
crescendo
rit.
con-ta-mi-na-ted soils as if we were vic-tims of a force ma-jeure.
Sop
Alto
Ten
Bass
Fl.
Ob.
B♭ Cl.
Bsn.
B♭ Tpt.
Hn.
Tbn.
Timp.
tr
ff
Vln I
Vln II
Vla
Vlc
Bass

160
Solo
Sop
Alto
Ten
Bass
160
always accented
Fl.
ff
always accented
Ob.
ff
always accented
B♭ Cl.
ff
always accented
Bsn.
160
ff
always accented
B♭ Tpt.
ff
always accented
Hn.
ff
always accented
Tbn.
160
ff
always accented
Timp.
160
always accented
Vln I
ff
always accented
Vln II
fff
always accented
Vla
ff
always accented
Vlc
ff
arco
always accented
Bass
ff

162
Solo
Sop
Alto
Ten
Bass
162
Fl.
Ob.
B♭ Cl.
Bsn.
162
B♭ Tpt.
Hn.
Tbn.
162
Timp.
162
Vln I
Vln II
Vla
Vlc
Bass

165
Solo
Sop
Alto
Ten
Bass
(no rit.)
Fl.
Ob.
B♭ Cl.
Bsn.
B♭ Tpt.
Hn.
Tbn.
Timp.
Vln I
Vln II
Vla
Vlc
Bass
crescendo
subito p
ff
tr

168
♩= 92 Moderato
Solo
Sop
Alto
Ten
Bass
p
We have bare - ly a - ny tears a - ny
168
Fl.
Ob.
B♭ Cl.
Bsn.
168
B♭ Tpt.
Hn.
Tbn.
168
Timp.
168
Vln I
Vln II
Vla
Vlc
Bass

Sop: tears left for tran - si - ence it - self,

Alto: tears left for tran - si - ence it - self,

Ten: tears left for tran - si - ence it - self,

Bass: tears left for tran - si - ence it - self,

Sop/Alto/Ten/Bass: which used to touch us in the death of a com - mon

180
Solo
Sop
fly or the fall of a fledg-ling from its high nest.
Alto
fly or the fall of a fledg - - - - ling from its
Ten
fly or the fall of a fledg - - - - ling from its
Bass
180 fly or the fall of a fledg - - - - ling from its
Fl.
Ob.
B♭ Cl.
Bsn.
180
B♭ Tpt.
Hn.
Tbn.
180
Timp.
180
Vln I
Vln II
Vla
Vlc
Bass

184
Solo
Sop
mf
Or when the mount - tain stream car-ried off scree and peb - bles and
Alto
mf
nest. Or when the moun-tain stream car - ried peb - bles and
Ten
mf
nest. Or when the moun-tain stream car - ried peb - bles and
Bass
mf
nest. Or when the moun-tain stream car - ried peb - bles and
Fl.
Ob.
B♭ Cl.
Bsn.
B♭ Tpt.
Hn.
Tbn.
Timp.
Vln I
Vln II
Vla
Vlc
Bass

188
Solo
Sop
filled up- the lake that we chil - dren wished to be
Alto
filled up- the lake that we chil - dren wished
Ten
filled up- the lake that we chil - dren wished
Bass
filled up- the lake that we chil - dren wished
Fl.
Ob.
B♭ Cl.
Bsn.
B♭ Tpt.
Hn.
Tbn.
Timp.
Vln I
Vln II
Vla
Vlc
Bass

192
Solo
Sop
ev - er big and blue and ev - er - last - ing.
Alto
ev - er blue ev - er - last - ing.
Ten
ev - er blue ev - er - last - ing.
Bass
ev - er blue ev - er - last - ing.
192
Fl.
Ob.
B♭ Cl.
Bsn.
192
B♭ Tpt.
Hn.
Tbn.
192
Timp.
192
Vln I
Vln II
Vla
Vlc
Bass

196
rit.
Slower
♩= 88
Solo
Sop
Alto
Ten
Bass
decrescendo
p
ev - er - last - - - ing.
Tear-less we go on
Tear - less
Fl.
Ob.
B♭ Cl.
Bsn.
B♭ Tpt.
Hn.
Tbn.
Timp.
Vln I
Vln II
Vla
Vlc
Bass
decrescendo

200
Solo
Sop
Alto
Ten
Bass
crescendo
weep - - - ing for the deaths we have
weep - ing for the deaths we have
weep - - - ing for the deaths we have
weep - - - ing for the deaths we have
Fl.
Ob.
mp
B♭ Cl.
Bsn.
B♭ Tpt.
Hn.
Tbn.
Timp.
Vln I
Vln II
Vla
Vlc
Bass

204
Solo
Sop
Alto
Ten
Bass
mf
lived to see
and for the
Fl.
Ob.
B♭ Cl.
Bsn.
B♭ Tpt.
Hn.
Tbn.
Timp.
Vln I
Vln II
Vla
Vlc
Bass
mp

208
crescendo
Solo
Sop
Alto
Ten
Bass
death that is in store for us
Fl.
Ob.
B♭ Cl.
Bsn.
B♭ Tpt.
Hn.
Tbn.
Timp.
Vln I
Vln II
Vla
Vlc
Bass

212
♩= 84 Andante
Solo
Sop
Alto
Ten
Bass
Fl.
Ob.
B♭ Cl.
Bsn.
B♭ Tpt.
Hn.
Tbn.
Timp.
Vln I
Vln II
Vla
Vlc
Bass
all.
La - cri -
mp
tr
f
V

216
Solo
Sop
mo - sa di - es il - la qua re -
Alto
mo - sa di - es il - la qua re -
Ten
mo - sa di - es il - la qua re -
Bass
mo - sa di - es il - la qua re -
216
Fl.
(continue)
Ob.
(continue)
B♭ Cl.
Bsn.
216
B♭ Tpt.
Hn.
Tbn.
216
Timp.
216
Vln I
(continue)
Vln II
(continue)
Vla
Vlc
Bass

220
a tempo
poco rit.
mf
Solo
Ju -
Sop
Alto
Ten
Bass
sur - get ex fa - vil - la.
Fl.
Ob.
B♭ Cl.
Bsn.
B♭ Tpt.
Hn.
Tbn.
Timp.
Vln I
Vln II
Vla
Vlc
Bass
p

224
Solo
di - can - dus ho - mo re - - -
Sop
Alto
Ten
Bass
Fl.
Ob.
(continue)
B♭ Cl.
Bsn.
B♭ Tpt.
Hn.
Tbn.
Timp.
Vln I
Vln II
Vla
Vlc
Bass

179

IV. De profundo lacu

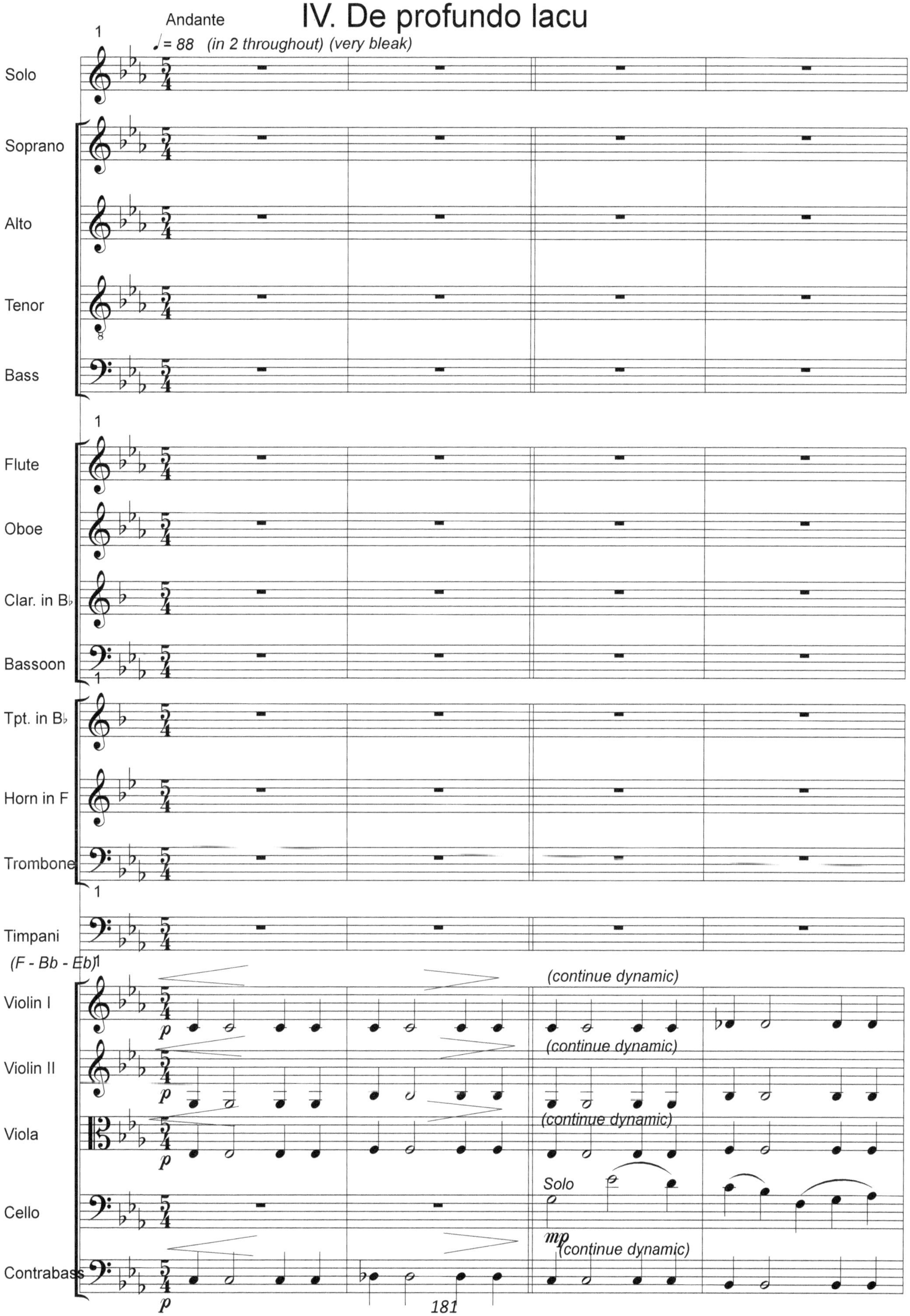

Requiem IV: De profundo lacu

182

9
poco rit.
dim.
a tempo
Solo
Sop
Alto
Ten
Bass
Fl.
Ob.
B♭ Cl.
Bsn.
B♭ Tpt.
Hn.
Tbn.
Timp.
Vln I
Vln II
Vla
Vlc
Bass
pp
mp

(renewed anguish)

184

17
Solo
Sop
Alto
Ten
Bass
17
Fl.
Ob.
B♭ Cl.
Bsn.
17
B♭ Tpt.
Hn.
Tbn.
17
Timp.
17
Vln I
Vln II
Vla
Vlc
Bass

(same tempo)

Sop: *pp* We weep un - til deep

Alto: *pp* We weep un - til deep

Ten: *pp* We weep un - til deep

Bass: We weep un - til deep

decrescendo

Vln I: *ppp*

Vln II: *ppp*

Vla: *ppp*

Vlc: *ppp*

Bass: *ppp*

25
poco rit.
Solo
Sop
in the night the ma - ny deaths con - dense in - to the
Alto
in the night the ma - ny deaths con - dense in - to the
Ten
in the night the ma - ny deaths con - dense in - to the
Bass
in the night the ma - ny deaths con - dense in - to the
Fl.
Ob.
B♭ Cl.
Bsn.
B♭ Tpt.
Hn.
Tbn.
Timp.
Vln I
Vln II
Vla
Vlc
Bass

Solo

Sop
one   dark   death,   whose   black - - - ness

Alto
one   dark   death,   whose   black - - ness

Ten
one   dark   death,   whose   black - - - ness

Bass
one   dark   death,   whose   black - - - ness

Fl.

Ob.

B♭ Cl.

Bsn.

B♭ Tpt.

Hn.

Tbn.

Timp.

Vln I

Vln II

Vla

Vlc

Bass

33
rit.
Allegro
♩ = 140 with urgency
Solo
Sop
Alto
Ten
Bass
ppp (sotto voce)
swal - lows all. De poe - nis in - fer - ni et
Fl.
Ob.
B♭ Cl.
Bsn.
B♭ Tpt.
Hn.
Tbn.
Timp.
Vln I
Vln II
Vla
Vlc
Bass
pizzicato
ppp

37
Solo
Sop
de pro-fun - do la - cu “mi-se - re - re!“ sup-pli - ca - mus,
Alto
de pro-fun - do la - cu “mi-se - re - re!“ sup-pli - ca - mus,
Ten
de pro-fun - do la - cu “mi-se - re - re!“ sup-pli - ca - mus
Bass
de pro-fun - do la - cu “mi-se - re - re!“ sup-pli - ca - mus,
Fl.
Ob.
B♭ Cl.
Bsn.
B♭ Tpt.
Hn.
Tbn.
Timp.
Vln I
Vln II
Vla
Vlc
Bass

li - be - ra nos de o - re le - o - nis ne ca - da - mus

li - be - ra nos de o - re le - o - nis ne ca - da - mus

li - be - ra nos de o - re le - o - nis ne ca - da - mus

li - be - ra nos de o - re le - o - nis ne ca - da - mus

No light

in ob - scu - rum.

in ob - scu - rum.

in ob - scu - rum.

in ob - scu - rum.

192

pier - ces the gloom.

No   sun   nor

Solo: moon shines in - to the bot - - -

194

Solo

Sop

tom - less   pit.   *pp*

Alto

pp De   poe - nis   in -

Ten

pp De   poe - nis   in -

Bass

pp De   poe - nis   in -

De   poe - nis   in -

Fl.

Ob.

B♭ Cl.

Bsn.

B♭ Tpt.

Hn.

Tbn.

Timp.

Vln I

Vln II

Vla

Vlc

pp

Bass

pp

195

Sop: fer - ni et de pro - fun - do la - cu "mi - se - re - re!"
Alto: fer - ni et de pro - fun - do la - cu "mi - se - re - re!"
Ten: fer - ni et de pro - fun - do la - cu "mi - se - re - re!"
Bass: fer - ni et de pro - fun - do la - cu "mi - se - re - re!"

196

sup - pli - ca - mus, li - be - ra nos de o - re le - o - nis ne

sup - pli - ca - mus, li - be - ra nos de o - re le - o - nis ne

sup - pli - ca - mus li - be - ra nos de o - re le - o - nis ne

sup - pli - ca - mus, li - be - ra nos de o - re le - o - nis ne

197

Moderato
♩= 108
69
rit.
mp
Solo
Sop
ca - da - mus in ob - scu - rum.
Alto
ca - da - mus in ob - scu - rum.
Ten
ca - da - mus in ob - scu - rum.
Bass
ca - da - mus in ob - scu - rum.
Fl.
Ob.
B♭ Cl.
Bsn.
B♭ Tpt.
Hn.
Tbn.
Timp.
Vln I
Vln II
Vla
Vlc
Bass
p

Solo: No life pul - ses in the so - lid black-ness. No flap -

ping   wing   moves,

200

81
rit.
Allegro
♩ = 140
Solo
Sop
Alto
Ten
Bass
the emp - - - - - - - ty air.
mp
De
Fl.
Ob.
B♭ Cl.
Bsn.
B♭ Tpt.
Hn.
Tbn.
Timp.
Vln I
Vln II
Vla
Vlc
Bass

Requiem IV: De profundo lacu

poe - nis in - fer - ni et de pro - fun - do la - cu

202

Sop: "mi - se - re - re!" sup - pli - ca - mus, li - be - ra nos de o - re le -

Alto: "mi - se - re - re!" sup - pli - ca - mus, li - be - ra nos de o - re le -

Ten: "mi - se - re - re!" sup - pli - ca - mus li - be - ra nos de o - re le -

Bass: "mi - se - re - re!" sup - pli - ca - mus, li - be - ra nos de o - re le -

Requiem IV: De profundo lacu

Solo

Sop

o - nis ne ca - da - mus in ob - scu - rum.

Alto

o - nis ne ca - da - mus in ob - scu - rum.

Ten

o - nis ne ca - da - mus in ob - scu - rum.

Bass

o - nis ne ca - da - mus in ob - scu - rum.

Fl.

Ob.

B♭ Cl.

Bsn.

B♭ Tpt.

Hn.

Tbn.

Timp.

Vln I

Vln II

Vla

Vlc

Bass

204

Neither faith nor hope survive

Requiem IV: De profundo lacu

in such deep - ness, such deep - ness.

Veni Creator Spiritus

Rare is the love   that

Allegro
♩= 140
rit.
Solo
Sop
Alto
Ten
Bass
dares to go so far, so low.
De
Fl.
Ob.
B♭ Cl.
Bsn.
B♭ Tpt.
Hn.
Tbn.
Timp.
Vln I
Vln II
Vla
Vlc
Bass
crescendo
decrescendo
109

113
with urgency
Solo
Sop
poe - nis in - fer - ni et de pro - fun - do la - cu
Alto
poe - nis in - fer - ni et de pro - fun - do la - cu
Ten
poe - nis in - fer - ni et de pro - fun - do la - cu
Bass
113 poe - nis in - fer - ni et de pro - fun - do la - cu
Fl.
Ob.
B♭ Cl.
Bsn.
113
B♭ Tpt.
Hn.
Tbn.
113
Timp.
113
Vln I
Vln II
Vla
Vlc
Bass

Vocal text (Sop, Alto, Ten, Bass):
"mi - se - re - re!" sup - pli - ca - mus, li - be - ra nos de o - re le -

o - nis ne ca - da - mus in ob - scu - rum.

o - nis ne ca - da - mus in ob - scu - rum.

o - nis ne ca - da - mus in ob - scu - rum.

o - nis ne ca - da - mus in ob - scu - rum.

125
Solo
Sop
Alto
Ten
Bass
mp
And thus we plead
Fl.
Ob.
B♭ Cl.
Bsn.
B♭ Tpt.
Hn.
Tbn.
Timp.
Vln I
Vln II
Vla
Vlc
Bass
(continue)

129
Solo
Sop
in our des-pair for de-li - - - - ve-rance from our a -
Alto
in our des-pair for de-li - - - - ve-rance from our a
Ten
in our des-pair for de-li - - - - ve-rance from our a -
Bass
in our des-pair for de-li - - - - ve-rance from our a -
129
Fl.
Ob.
B♭ Cl.
Bsn.
129
B♭ Tpt.
Hn.
Tbn.
129
Timp.
129
Vln I
Vln II
Vla
Vlc
Bass

133
rit.
Solo
Sop
Alto
Ten
Bass
go - nies there in the depth where sea-weeds stran - gle our
Fl.
Ob.
B♭ Cl.
Bsn.
B♭ Tpt.
Hn.
Tbn.
Timp.
Vln I
Vln II
Vla
Vlc
Bass

137
Allegro
♩= 140
with urgency
Solo
Sop
Alto
Ten
Bass
crescendo
soul. De poe - nis in - fer - ni et de pro - fun - do
Fl.
Ob.
B♭ Cl.
Bsn.
B♭ Tpt.
Hn.
Tbn.
Timp.
Vln I
Vln II
Vla
Vlc
Bass
mp
f

141
Solo
Sop
la - cu "mi-se - re - re!" (♮) sup-pli - ca - mus, li - be - ra nos
Alto
la - cu "mi-se - re - re!" sup-pli - ca - mus, li - be - ra nos
Ten
la - cu "mi-se - re - re!" sup-pli - ca - mus li - be - ra nos
Bass
la - cu "mi-se - re - re!" sup-pli - ca - mus, li - be - ra nos
Fl.
Ob.
B♭ Cl.
Bsn.
B♭ Tpt.
Hn.
Tbn.
Timp.
Vln I
Vln II
Vla
Vlc
Bass

145
Solo
Sop
de o - re le - o - nis ne ca - da - mus in ob - scu - rum.
Alto
de o - re le - o - nis ne ca - da - mus in ob - scu - rum.
Ten
de o - re le - o - nis ne ca - da - mus in ob - scu - rum.
Bass
de o - re le - o - nis ne ca - da - mus in ob - scu - rum.
Fl.
Ob.
B♭ Cl.
Bsn.
B♭ Tpt.
Hn.
Tbn.
Timp.
Vln I
Vln II
Vla
Vlc
Bass

149
Allegro
♩= 124
ff with urgency
Solo
Sop
Alto
Ten
Bass
We cry to God, to our
We cry to God, to our
We cry to God, to our
We cry to God, to our
We cry to God, to our
Fl.
Ob.
B♭ Cl.
Bsn.
B♭ Tpt.
Hn.
Tbn.
Timp.
Vln I
Vln II
Vla
Vlc
Bass
mf
crescendo
ff

153
Solo
mo - thers, to life it - self: De - li - ver
Sop
mo - thers, to life it - self: De - li - ver
Alto
mo - thers, to life it - self, De - li - ver
Ten
mo - thers, to life it - self, De - li - ver
Bass
mo - thers, to life it - self, De - li - ver
Fl.
Ob.
B♭ Cl.
Bsn.
B♭ Tpt.
Hn.
Tbn.
Timp.
Vln I
Vln II
Vla
Vlc
Bass

crescendo   *accel.*

Solo

Sop

us   from the   jaws   of the   li - - - on,

Alto

us   from the   jaws   of the   li - - - on,

Ten

us   from the   jaws   of the   li - - - on,

Bass

us   from the   jaws   of the   li - - - on,

Fl.

Ob.

B♭ Cl.

Bsn.

B♭ Tpt.

Hn.

Tbn.

Timp.

Vln I

Vln II

Vla

Vlc

Bass

220

161
Allegro
♩= 140 with urgency
Solo
Sop
Alto
Ten
Bass
Fl.
Ob.
B♭ Cl.
Bsn.
B♭ Tpt.
Hn.
Tbn.
Timp.
tr
Vln I
Vln II
Vla
Vlc
Bass
(off-string near frog)
ff

222

Andante
169
no rit.
mp ♩= 80
Solo
Sop
Alto
Ten
Bass
and let us not
and let us not
on, and let us
on, and let us
and let us not
Fl.
Ob.
B♭ Cl.
Bsn.
B♭ Tpt.
Hn.
Tbn.
Timp.
crescendo
Vln I
Vln II
Vla
Vlc
Bass

173
Adagio
♩= 60
♩= 92 Andante
Solo
Sop
Alto
Ten
Bass
fall in - to dark - ness!
Fl.
Ob.
B♭ Cl.
Bsn.
B♭ Tpt.
Hn.
Tbn.
Timp.
Vln I
Vln II
Vla
Vlc
Bass
molto legato
Solo
p

177
Solo
Sop
Alto
Ten
Bass
177
Fl.
Ob.
B♭ Cl.
Bsn.
177
B♭ Tpt.
Veni Creator Spiritus
with mute
Hn.
p
Tbn.
177
Timp.
177
Vln I
Vln II
Vla
molto legato
Vlc
mp
Bass

226

185
Solo
Sop
Alto
Ten
Bass
185
Fl.
molto legato
p
Ob.
molto legato
p
B♭ Cl.
molto legato
p
Bsn.
molto legato
p
185
B♭ Tpt.
Hn.
Tbn.
185
Timp.
185
Vln I
Vln II
Vla
Vlc
Bass

189
Solo
Sop
Alto
Ten
Bass
189
Fl.
Ob.
B♭ Cl.
Bsn.
189
B♭ Tpt.
Hn.
Tbn.
189
Timp.
189
Vln I
Vln II
Vla
Vlc
Bass

193
rit.
Solo
Sop
Alto
Ten
Bass
193
Fl.
Ob.
B♭ Cl.
Bsn.
193
B♭ Tpt.
Hn.
Tbn.
193
Timp.
193
Vln I
Vln II
Vla
3
Vlc
Bass

V. Hosanna in excelsis

Sop. / Alto: When we may weep a - gain, may

Alto: When we may weep a - gain,

Ten.: When we may weep a - gain,

Bass: When we may weep a - gain,

weep a - gain, weep a - gain, be -

weep a - gain, weep a - gain, be -

weep a - gain, weep a - gain, be -

weep a - gain, weep a - gain, be -

13
Solo
Sop.
gins the re - sur - rec - tion,
Alto
gins the re - sur - rec - tion,
Ten.
gins the re - sur - rec - tion,
Bass
13 gins the re - sur - rec - tion,
Fl.
Ob.
B♭ Cl.
Bsn.
13
B♭ Tpt.
Hn.
Tbn.
13
Vln I
Vln II
Vla
Vlc
Bass

17
Solo
Sop.
be - - - - - gins, be - - - - - gins the
Alto
be - - - - - gins, be - - - - - gins the
Ten.
be - - - - - gins, be - - - - - gins the
Bass
17 be - - - - - gins, be - - - - - gins the
Fl.
Ob.
B♭ Cl.
Bsn.
17
B♭ Tpt.
Hn.
Tbn.
17
Vln I
Vln II
Vla
Vlc
Bass

21
Soprano solo mp
(same tempo)
Solo
Ho - - - - -
Sop.
re - sur - rec - - - - tion.
Alto
re - sur - rec - - - - tion.
Ten.
re - sur - rec - - - - tion.
Bass
re - sur - rec - - - - tion.
Fl.
Ob.
B♭ Cl.
Bsn.
B♭ Tpt.
Hn.
Tbn.
Vln I
Vln II
Vla
Vlc
Bass
mp

25
Solo
san - na, ho - - - - - san - - na, ho - - - -
Sop.
Alto
Ten.
Bass
25
Fl.
Ob.
B♭ Cl.
Bsn.
25
B♭ Tpt.
Hn.
Tbn.
25
Vln I
Vln II
Vla
Vlc
Bass

san - - na, ho - san - - na, in ex -

cel - - - sis!

239

37
Slower
♩= 104
poco rit.
Solo
Sop.
Alto
Ten.
Bass
p
When we
When we
When we
When we
Fl.
Ob.
B♭ Cl.
Bsn.
B♭ Tpt.
Hn.
Tbn.
Vln I
Vln II
Vla
Vlc
Bass
decrescendo

41
Solo
Sop.
weep,
weep,
Alto
weep,
weep,
Ten.
weep,
weep,
Bass
weep,
weep,
Fl.
Ob.
B♭ Cl.
Bsn.
B♭ Tpt.
Hn.
Tbn.
Vln I
Vln II
Vla
Vlc
Bass

when we weep

when we weep

when we weep

when we weep

49
accel.
Faster
♩= 108
Solo
Sop.
mf
we can re - turn
Alto
mf
we can re - turn
Ten.
mf
we can re - turn
Bass
mf
we can re - turn
Fl.
mf
Ob.
B♭ Cl.
Bsn.
B♭ Tpt.
Hn.
Tbn.
Vln I
mf
Vln II
Vla
Vlc
mp
Bass

53
Solo
Sop.
to
life,
Alto
to
life,
Ten.
to
life,
Bass
to
life,
53
Fl.
Ob.
B♭ Cl.
Bsn.
53
B♭ Tpt.
Hn.
Tbn.
53
Vln I
Vln II
Vla
Vlc
Bass

57
Solo
Sop.
re - turn to life.
Alto
re - turn to life.
Ten.
re - turn to life.
Bass
re - turn to life.
Fl.
Ob.
B♭ Cl.
Bsn.
B♭ Tpt.
Hn.
Tbn.
Vln I
Vln II
Vla
Vlc
Bass

61
(same tempo)
Solo
Ho - - - - - san - na, ho - - - - -
decrescendo
Sop.
Alto
Ten.
Bass
Fl.
Ob.
B♭ Cl.
Bsn.
B♭ Tpt.
Hn.
Tbn.
Vln I
Vln II
Vla
Vlc
decrescendo
Bass

65
Solo
san - na, ho - - - - san - - - - - na, ho -
Sop.
Alto
Ten.
Bass
65
Fl.
Ob.
B♭ Cl.
Bsn.
65
B♭ Tpt.
Tbn.
65
Vln I
Vln II
Vla
Vlc
Bass

san - na   in   ex - - cel - - - - sis!

73
(no rit.)
(same tempo)
Solo
Sop.
Alto
Ten.
Bass
73
Fl.
Ob.
B♭ Cl.
Bsn.
mp
mp
Solo
mf
73
B♭ Tpt.
Hn.
Tbn.
73
Vln I
Vln II
Vla
Vlc
Bass
mp
mp
mp
mp

77
Solo
Sop.
Alto
Ten.
Bass
Fl.
Ob.
B♭ Cl.
Bsn.
B♭ Tpt.
Hn.
Tbn.
Vln I
Vln II
Vla
Vlc
Bass

81
Solo
Sop.
Alto
Ten.
Bass
81
Fl.
Ob.
B♭ Cl.
Bsn.
81
B♭ Tpt.
Hn.
Tbn.
81
Vln I
Vln II
Vla
Vlc
Bass

85
Solo
Sop.
Alto
Ten.
Bass
85
Fl.
Ob.
B♭ Cl.
Bsn.
85
B♭ Tpt.
Hn.
Tbn.
85
Vln I
Vln II
Vla
Vlc
Bass

89
rit.
Moderato
♩= 100 (in 2)
Solo
Sop.
mp
When we
Alto
Ten.
Bass
Fl.
Ob.
B♭ Cl.
Bsn.
B♭ Tpt.
Hn.
Tbn.
legato
Vln I
Vln II
Vla
Vlc
Bass
p

93
Solo
Sop.
weep with those who weep, with
Alto
mp
When we
Ten.
Bass
93
Fl.
Ob.
B♭ Cl.
Bsn.
93
B♭ Tpt.
Hn.
Tbn.
93
Vln I
Vln II
Vla
Vlc
Bass
p

97
Solo
Sop.
those with those who weep with those
Alto
weep with those who weep, with those
Ten.
Bass
97
Fl.
Ob.
B♭ Cl.
Bsn.
97
B♭ Tpt.
Hn.
Tbn.
97
Vln I
Vln II
Vla
Vlc
Bass

101
Solo
Sop.
with
those
who
weep,
with
Alto
with
those
who
weep,
with
Ten.
mp
When
we
weep
with
those
who
Bass
101
Fl.
Ob.
B♭ Cl.
Bsn.
101
B♭ Tpt.
Hn.
Tbn.
101
Vln I
p
Vln II
p
Vla
p
Vlc
p
Bass
p

105
Solo
Sop.
those
who
weep,
When
we
Alto
those
who
weep,
who
Ten.
weep,
we
weep
with
those
who
Bass
mp
When
we
weep
with
those
who
Fl.
Ob.
B♭ Cl.
Bsn.
B♭ Tpt.
Hn.
Tbn.
Vln I
p
Vln II
p
Vla
p
Vlc
p
Bass
p

Faster
♩= 108
109
Solo
Sop.
Alto
Ten.
Bass
Fl.
Ob.
B♭ Cl.
Bsn.
B♭ Tpt.
Hn.
Tbn.
Vln I
Vln II
Vla
Vlc
Bass
weep those who re -
weep, those who re -
weep, those who re -
weep, those who re -
mf
crescendo

Lyrics visible in the vocal parts:

Sop.: joice, those who re-joice will give us
Alto: joice, those who re-joice, will give us
Ten.: joice, those who re-joice, will give us
Bass: joice, those who re-joice, will give us

117
molto rit.
Slower
♩= 100
Solo
Sop.
Alto
Ten.
Bass
decrescendo
mp
mf
When we
joy!
Weep,
joy |
When we weep with those who
Fl.
Ob.
B♭ Cl.
Bsn.
B♭ Tpt.
Hn.
Tbn.
Vln I
Vln II
Vla
Vlc
Bass
p

121
Solo
weep,
weep
with
Sop.
we
weep
with
Alto
weep,
weep
with
those
who
Ten.
we
weep
Bass
121
When
we
weep
with
those
who
Fl.
Ob.
B♭ Cl.
Bsn.
121
B♭ Tpt.
Hn.
Tbn.
121
Vln I
Vln II
Vla
Vlc
Bass

125
Solo
those
those
who
Sop.
those
who
weep,
When
we
Alto
weep,
with
those
who
weep,
who
Ten.
with
those
who
weep,
who
Bass
weep,
those
who
weep,
who
Fl.
Ob.
B♭ Cl.
Bsn.
B♭ Tpt.
Hn.
Tbn.
Vln I
Vln II
Vla
Vlc
Bass

129
Solo
weep, we weep we
Sop.
weep with those who weep, we
Alto
weep, with those who
Ten.
weep, When we
Bass
129 weep, with those who
Fl.
Ob.
B♭ Cl.
Bsn.
129
B♭ Tpt.
Hn.
Tbn.
129
Vln I
Vln II
Vla
Vlc
Bass

Faster
♩= 108
accel.
133
crescendo
Solo
weep with those who weep, those
Sop.
weep with those who weep, those
Alto
weep, When we weep, those
Ten.
weep with those who weep, those
Bass
weep, who weep, those
Fl.
Ob.
B♭ Cl.
Bsn.
B♭ Tpt.
Hn.
Tbn.
Vln I
Vln II
Vla
Vlc
Bass
mf

137
Solo
who re - joice, those who re -
Sop.
who re - joice, those who re -
Alto
who re - - -joice, those who re -
Ten.
who re - joice, those who re -
Bass
who re - joice, those who re -
137
Fl.
Ob.
B♭ Cl.
Bsn.
137
B♭ Tpt.
Hn.
Tbn.
137
Vln I
Vln II
Vla
Vlc
Bass

Faster
♩= 116
(in 2)
141
accel.
Solo
joice will give us joy!
Sop.
joice will give us joy!
Alto
joice will give us joy!
Ten.
joice will give us joy!
those who re -
Bass
joice will give us joy!
Fl.
Ob.
B♭ Cl.
Bsn.
B♭ Tpt.
Hn.
Tbn.
Vln I
Vln II
Vla
Vlc
Bass
f
mf
mp

145
Solo
Sop.
mf
those who re -
Alto
Ten.
joice, will give us joy |
Bass
145
Fl.
Ob.
B♭ Cl.
Bsn.
145
B♭ Tpt.
mp
Hn.
Tbn.
145
Vln I
Vln II
Vla
Vlc
Bass

149
Solo
Sop.
joice, will give us joy | will
Alto
Ten.
those who re - joice, re - - joice will
Bass
mf
those who re -
149
Fl.
Ob.
B♭ Cl.
Bsn.
149
B♭ Tpt.
Hn.
Tbn.
mp
149
Vln I
Vln II
Vla
Vlc
Bass

153
Solo
Sop.
give us joy! will give us joy! those who re -
Alto
mf
those who re -
Ten.
give us joy! those who re -
Bass
joice will give us joy! who re -
Fl.
Ob.
B♭ Cl.
mp
Bsn.
B♭ Tpt.
Hn.
Tbn.
Vln I
Vln II
Vla
Vlc
Bass

157
rit.
Slower
♩= 100
Solo
Sop.
Alto
Ten.
Bass
mf
mf When we
joice will give us joy!
mf When we
joice will give us joy!
mf When we
joice will give us joy!
mf When we
157 joice will give us joy! When we
Fl.
Ob.
B♭ Cl.
Bsn.
157
B♭ Tpt.
Hn.
Tbn.
157
Vln I
Vln II
Vla
Vlc
Bass
mp

161
Solo
weep when we weep we
Sop.
weep, when we weep,
Alto
weep, when we weep,
Ten.
weep, when we weep,
Bass
weep, when we weep,
Fl.
Ob.
B♭ Cl.
Bsn.
B♭ Tpt.
Hn.
Tbn.
Vln I
Vln II
Vla
Vlc
Bass

165
Solo
Sop.
Alto
Ten.
Bass
weep
when we weep,
with those who
165
Fl.
Ob.
B♭ Cl.
Bsn.
165
B♭ Tpt.
Hn.
Tbn.
165
Vln I
Vln II
Vla
Vlc
Bass

169
Solo
subito
f
weep,
those
who
re - joice,
Sop.
Alto
Ten.
Bass
Fl.
mf
Ob.
B♭ Cl.
Bsn.
B♭ Tpt.
Hn.
Tbn.
Vln I
Vln II
Vla
Vlc
Bass

173
rit.
Solo
will give us
Sop.
will give us joy |
Alto
will give us joy |
Ten.
will give us joy |
Bass
will give us joy |
Fl.
Ob.
B♭ Cl.
Bsn.
B♭ Tpt.
Hn.
Tbn.
Vln I
Vln II
Vla
Vlc
Bass

Moderato ♩= 116 (in 3)
177
Solo
joy
Ho - - - - san - na, ho - - -
Sop.
Alto
Ten.
Bass
Fl.
Ob.
B♭ Cl.
Bsn.
B♭ Tpt.
Hn.
Tbn.
Vln I
Vln II
Vla
Vlc
Bass

san - na, ho - - - san - - na, ho -

185
Solo
san - na in ex - cel - - - - sis!
Sop.
Alto
Ten.
Bass
185
Fl.
Ob.
B♭ Cl.
Bsn.
185
B♭ Tpt.
Hn.
Tbn.
185
Vln I
Vln II
Vla
Vlc
Bass

189
(no rit.)
(same tempo)
Solo
Sop.
Ple - ni sunt coe - - -
Alto
Ple - ni sunt coe - - -
Ten.
Ple - ni sunt coe - - -
Bass
Ple - ni sunt coe - - -
Fl.
Ob.
crescendo
B♭ Cl.
Bsn.
B♭ Tpt.
Hn.
Tbn.
Vln I
Vln II
crescendo
Vla
Vlc
Bass

193
Solo
Sop.
li et ter - - - - ra glo - ri -
Alto
li et ter - - - - ra glo - ri -
Ten.
li et ter - - - - ra glo - ri -
Bass
li et ter - - - - ra glo - ri -
193
Fl.
Ob.
B♭ Cl.
Bsn.
193
B♭ Tpt.
Hn.
Tbn.
193
Vln I
Vln II
Vla
Vlc
Bass

197
Solo
Sop.
Alto
Ten.
Bass
a
a
a
a
glo
glo
glo
glo
Fl.
Ob.
B♭ Cl.
Bsn.
B♭ Tpt.
Hn.
mf
Tbn.
Vln I
Vln II
Vla
Vlc
Bass

201
Solo
Sop.
ri - a magni - - - -
Alto
ri - a mag - ni - - - -
Ten.
ri - a mag - ni - - - -
Bass
ri - a mag - ni - - - -
201
Fl.
Ob.
B♭ Cl.
Bsn.
201
B♭ Tpt.
Hn.
Tbn.
201
Vln I
Vln II
Vla
Vlc
Bass

205
Solo
Sop.
fi - ca mag - ni - - - - -
Alto
fi - ca mag - ni - - - - -
Ten.
fi - ca mag - ni - - - - -
Bass
205
fi - ca mag - ni - - - - -
Fl.
Ob.
B♭ Cl.
Bsn.
205
B♭ Tpt.
Hn.
Tbn.
205
Vln I
Vln II
Vla
Vlc
Bass

209
Solo soprano
Solo
Ho - - -
Sop.
fi - ca
Alto
fi - ca
Ten.
fi - ca
Bass
fi - ca
209
crescendo
Fl.
Ob.
B♭ Cl.
Bsn.
209
B♭ Tpt.
Hn.
Tbn.
209
crescendo
Vln I
Vln II
Vla
Vlc
Bass

san - na, ho - - - san - na, ho - - -

san - - - na,   ho - san - na   in   ex -

(same tempo)
(with Soprano 1)
221
Solo
cel - - - - - sis!
Ho - - - - -
Soprano 2
Sop.
Ho - - - - -
Alto
Ho - - - - -
Ten.
Ho - - - - -
Bass
Ho - - - - -
mf
221
Fl.
Ob.
B♭ Cl.
Bsn.
221
B♭ Tpt.
Hn.
Tbn.
mp
221
Vln I
Vln II
Vla
Vlc
Bass

225
Solo
san - na, ho - - - - - san - na, ho - - -
Sop.
san - na, ho - - - - - san - na, ho - - -
Alto
san - na, ho - - - - - san - na, ho - - -
Ten.
san - na, ho - - - - - san - na, ho - - -
Bass
225
san - - - - na, ho - - -
Fl.
Ob.
B♭ Cl.
Bsn.
225
B♭ Tpt.
Hn.
Tbn.
225
Vln I
Vln II
Vla
Vlc
Bass

229
decrescendo
Solo
san - na, ho - - - - san - na, ho - -
Sop.
san - na, ho - - - - san - na ho - -
Alto
san - na, ho - - - - san - - na, ho - -
Ten.
san - na, ho - - - - san - - na, ho - -
Bass
229 san - - - - - na, ho - -
Fl.
Ob.
B♭ Cl.
Bsn.
B♭ Tpt.
Hn.
Tbn.
Vln I
Vln II
Vla
Vlc
Bass

233
Solo
Sop.
Alto
Ten.
Bass
san - - - - na in ex - cel -
mp
decrescendo
Fl.
Ob.
B♭ Cl.
Bsn.
B♭ Tpt.
Hn.
Tbn.
p
Vln I
Vln II
Vla
Vlc
Bass

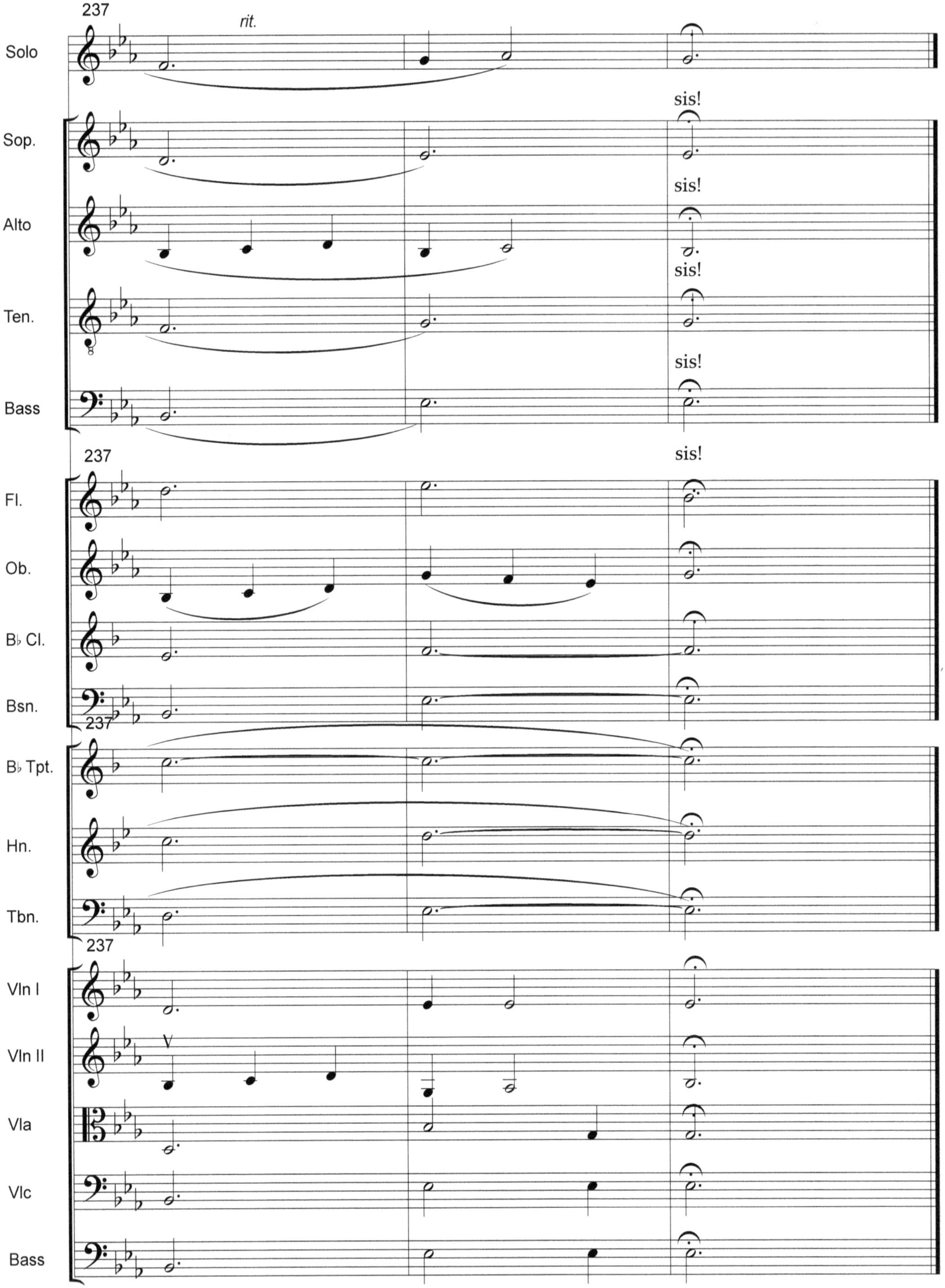
237
rit.
Solo
sis!
Sop.
sis!
Alto
sis!
Ten.
sis!
Bass
237
sis!
Fl.
Ob.
B♭ Cl.
Bsn.
237
B♭ Tpt.
Hn.
Tbn.
237
Vln I
Vln II
Vla
Vlc
Bass

Andante ♩= 88

VI. Qui tollit peccata mundi?

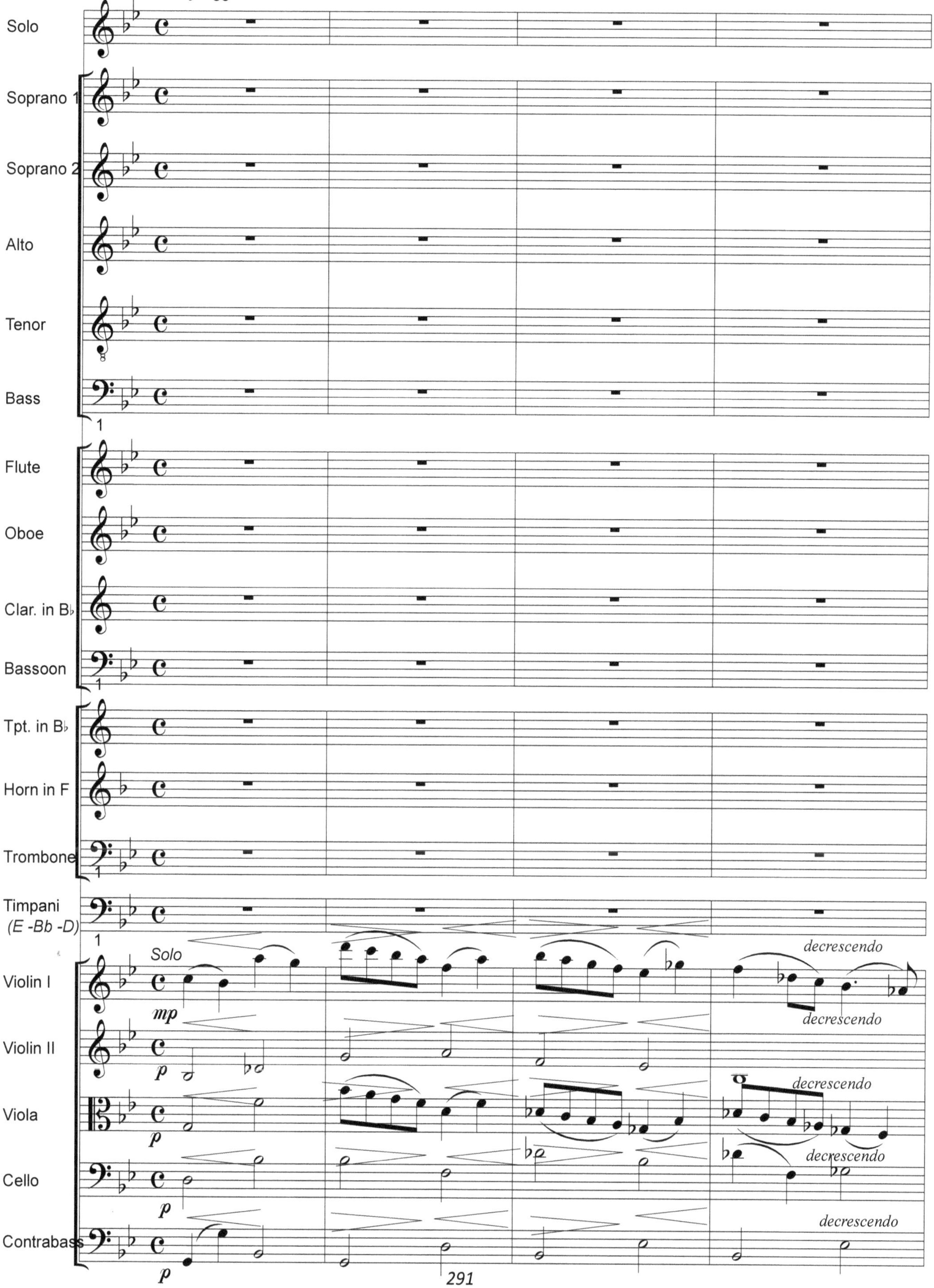

5
Solo
Sop 1
Sop 2
Alto
Ten
Bass
5
Fl.
Ob.
B♭ Cl.
Bsn.
5
B♭ Tpt.
Hn.
Tbn.
5
Timp.
5
Vln I
Vln II
Vla
Vlc
Bass
crescendo
crescendo
crescendo
crescendo
crescendo
p
p
mp
mp

(Solo Soprano)
9
Solo
Sop 1
Sop 2
Alto
Ten
Bass
Fl.
Ob.
B♭ Cl.
Bsn.
B♭ Tpt.
Hn.
Tbn.
Timp.
Vln I
Vln II
Vla
Vlc
Bass
decrescendo
pp

13
Solo
mf
Ag - nus De - i, qui tol - lis pec-ca - ta mun - di,
Sop 1
Sop 2
Alto
Ten
Bass
Fl.
Ob.
B♭ Cl.
Bsn.
B♭ Tpt.
Hn.
Tbn.
Timp.
Vln I
Vln II
Vla
Vlc
Bass
mp
p
crescendo
decrescendo

17
Solo
Ag - - - nus De - - - i, Ag - nus
Sop 1
Sop 2
Alto
Ten
Bass
Fl.
Ob.
B♭ Cl.
Bsn.
B♭ Tpt.
Hn.
Tbn.
Timp.
Vln I
Vln II
Vla
Vlc
Bass
crescendo
decrescendo
p

De - i, Ag - nus De - i, qui tol - lis pec -

297

298

no - bis do - na no - bis do - na

no - bis re - qui - em. do - na no - - - -

300

41
Solo
bis
re - qui - em.
Sop 1
Sop 2
Alto
Ten
Bass
Fl.
Ob.
B♭ Cl.
Bsn.
B♭ Tpt.
Hn.
Tbn.
Timp.
Vln I
(Solo)
mp
Vln II
p
Vla
Vlc
Bass

45
Solo
Sop 1
Sop 2
Alto
Ten
Bass
45
Fl.
Ob.
B♭ Cl.
Bsn.
45
B♭ Tpt.
Hn.
Tbn.
45
Timp.
45
Vln I
Vln II
Vla
Vlc
Bass
decrescendo
decrescendo
decrescendo
decrescendo
decrescendo

303

53
rit.
Slower
♩ = 84
Solo
Sop 1
Sop 2
Alto
Ten
Bass
mp
And if there is no
Fl.
Ob.
B♭ Cl.
Bsn.
B♭ Tpt.
Hn.
Tbn.
Timp.
Vln I
Vln II
Vla
Vlc
Bass
decrescendo
p

Sop 1: sa - cri - fi - cial lamb to take on the sins of the
Sop 2: sa - cri - fi - cial lamb to take on the sins of the
Alto: sa - cri - fi - cial lamb to take on the sins of the
Ten: sa - cri - fi - cial lamb to take on the sins of the
Bass: sa - cri - fi - cial lamb to take on the sins of the

world and give us e - - - ver - las - ting

world and give us e - ver - las - ting

world and give us e - ver - las - ting

world and give us e - ver - las - ting

world and give us e - ver - las - ting

65
Faster
♩= 92
Solo
Sop 1
Sop 2
Alto
Ten
Bass
Fl.
Ob.
B♭ Cl.
Bsn.
B♭ Tpt.
Hn.
Tbn.
Timp.
Vln I
Vln II
Vla
Vlc
Bass
pp
crescendo
mf
peace?
If there is none but we, the

69
Solo
Sop 1
Sop 2
Alto
Ten
Bass
crescendo
f
subito mp
wee - ping and the re - joi - - - cing and the faith in our
Fl.
Ob.
B♭ Cl.
Bsn.
B♭ Tpt.
Hn.
Tbn.
Timp.
Vln I
Vln II
Vla
Vlc
Bass
subito p

73
rit.
Solo
Sop 1
gra - cious bond?
Sop 2
gra - cious bond?
Alto
gra - cious bond?
Ten
gra - cious bond?
Bass
gra - cious bond?
Fl.
p
Ob.
p
B♭ Cl.
p
Bsn.
p
B♭ Tpt.
Hn.
p
Tbn.
Timp.
rit.
Vln I
Vln II
Vla
Vlc
Bass

77
Solo
Sop 1
Sop 2
Alto
Ten
Bass
Fl.
Ob.
B♭ Cl.
Bsn.
B♭ Tpt.
Hn.
Tbn.
Timp.
Vln I
Vln II
Vla
Vlc
Bass

81
rit.
♩= 88 Slower
Solo
Sop 1
Sop 2
Alto
Ten
Bass
mp
Will
Fl.
Ob.
B♭ Cl.
Bsn.
B♭ Tpt.
Hn.
Tbn.
Timp.
Vln I
Vln II
Vla
Vlc
Bass
p

Requiem VI: Qui tollit

we find ease in our - selves, in

we find ease in our - selves, in

we find ease in our - selves, in

we find ease in our - selves, in

we find ease in our - selves, in

312

89
rit.
Solo
Sop 1
o - thers in the world we have cre - a - ted?
Sop 2
o - thers in the world we have cre - a - ted?
Alto
o - thers in the world we have cre - a - ted?
Ten
o - thers in the world we have cre - a - ted?
Bass
o - thers in the world we have cre - a - ted?
Fl.
Ob.
B♭ Cl.
Bsn.
B♭ Tpt.
Hn.
Tbn.
Timp.
Vln I
Vln II
Vla
Vlc
Bass

Are we rea - dy to ac - cept its

97
molto rit.
Slower
♩= 88
Solo
Sop 1
Sop 2
Alto
Ten
Bass
blame and beau - - - - - ty in full
Fl.
Ob.
B♭ Cl.
Bsn.
B♭ Tpt.
Hn.
Tbn.
Timp.
Vln I
Vln II
Vla
Vlc
Bass
ff
mp

Faster
♩= 92
101
rit.
Solo
crescendo
ff
Sop 1
mag - ni - tude?
Sop 2
mag - ni - tude?
Alto
mag - ni - tude?
Ten
mag - ni - tude?
Bass
mag - ni - tude?
Fl.
Ob.
B♭ Cl.
Bsn.
B♭ Tpt.
Hn.
Tbn.
Timp.
Vln I
Vln II
Vla
Vlc
Bass

105
rit.
Solo
Sop 1
Sop 2
Alto
Ten
Bass
Fl.
Ob.
B♭ Cl.
Bsn.
B♭ Tpt.
Hn.
Tbn.
Timp.
Vln I
Vln II
Vla
Vlc
Bass

Andante
♩ = 88
109
Solo
Sop 1
Sop 2
Alto
Ten
Bass
Qui tol - - - lit Qui
rit.
Fl.
Ob.
B♭ Cl.
Bsn.
B♭ Tpt.
Hn.
Tbn.
Timp.
Vln I
Vln II
Vla
Vlc
Bass

319

117
Solo
Sop 1
Sop 2
Alto
Ten
Bass
lit Qui tol - - - lit Qui
lit Qui tol - - - lit Qui
lit Qui tol - - - lit Qui
lit Qui tol - - - lit Qui
lit Qui tol - - - lit Qui
lit Qui tol - - - lit Qui
Fl.
Ob.
B♭ Cl.
Bsn.
B♭ Tpt.
Hn.
Tbn.
Timp.
Vln I
Vln II
Vla
Vlc
Bass
p
p

121
Solo
tol - lit pec - ca - ta Qui tol - lit pec -
Sop 1
tol - lit pec - ca - ta Qui tol - lis pec -
Sop 2
tol - lit pec - ca - ta Qui tol - lit pec -
Alto
tol - lit pec - ca - ta Qui tol - lit pec -
Ten
tol - lit pec - ca - ta Qui tol - lit pec -
Bass
tol - lit pec - ca - ta Qui tol - lit pec -
Fl.
Ob.
B♭ Cl.
Bsn.
B♭ Tpt.
Hn.
Tbn.
Timp.
Vln I
Vln II
Vla
Vlc
Bass

125
rit.
decrescendo
Slower
♩= 84
Solo
Sop 1
Sop 2
Alto
Ten
Bass
ca - - ta mun - di? Do - - - na
Do - - - na nobis
Fl.
Ob.
B♭ Cl.
Bsn.
B♭ Tpt.
Hn.
Tbn.
Timp.
Vln I
Vln II
Vla
Vlc
Bass

129
Solo
Sop 1
Sop 2
Alto
Ten
Bass
Do - na no - bis Do - na no - bis
Fl.
Ob.
B♭ Cl.
Bsn.
B♭ Tpt.
Hn.
Tbn.
Timp.
Vln I
Vln II
Vla
Vlc
Bass

133
crescendo
mf
Solo
Sop 1
Sop 2
Alto
Ten
Bass
Do - na no - bis re -
Do - na no - bis re -
Do - na no - bis Do - na
Do - na no - bis re -
Do - na no - bis Do - na
Fl.
Ob.
B♭ Cl.
Bsn.
B♭ Tpt.
Hn.
Tbn.
Timp.
Vln I
Vln II
Vla
Vlc
Bass
p

137
rit.
decrescendo
Solo
qui - em.
re - - - qui - - - -
Sop 1
qui - em.
re - - - qui - - - -
Sop 2
no - - - - - - bis
re - - - qui - - - -
Alto
qui - em.
re - - - qui - -
Ten
no - - - - - - bis
re - qui -
Bass
qui - em.
re - - - qui - - - -
Fl.
Ob.
B♭ Cl.
Bsn.
B♭ Tpt.
Hn.
Tbn.
Timp.
Vln I
Vln II
Vla
Vlc
Bass

Requiem VI: Qui tollit

145
rit.
Solo
Sop 1
Sop 2
Alto
Ten
Bass
Fl.
Ob.
B♭ Cl.
Bsn.
B♭ Tpt.
Hn.
Tbn.
Timp.
Vln I
Vln II
Vla
Vlc
Bass
decrescendo
pp

VII. Lux perpetua

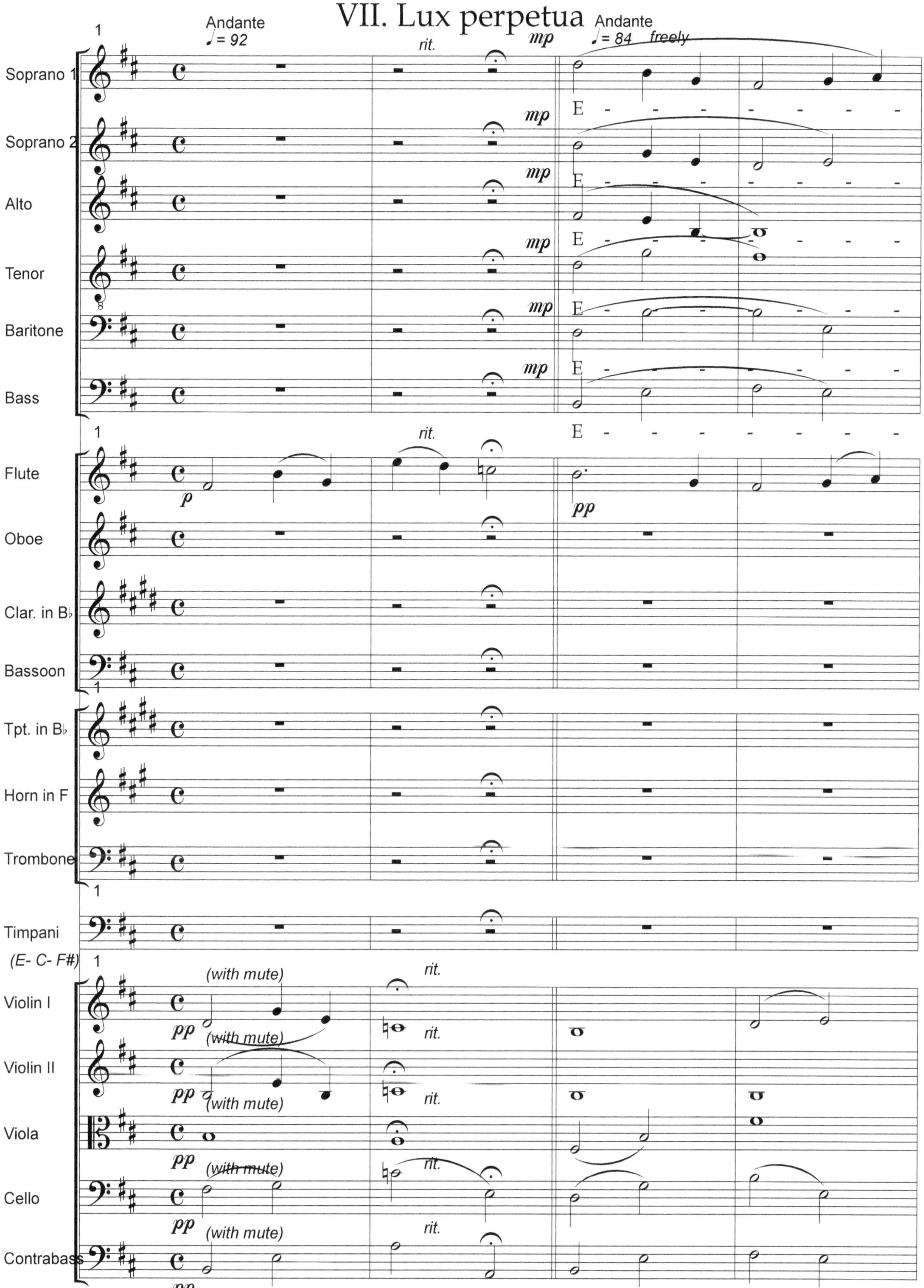

5
Sop 1
Sop 2
Alto
Ten
Bar
Bass
le - - - i - son,
e - - - - - - - -
mf
Fl.
Ob.
B♭ Cl.
Bsn.
B♭ Tpt.
Hn.
Tbn.
Timp.
Vln I
Vln II
Vla
Vlc
Bass
mp
p

9
Sop 1
Sop 2
Alto
Ten
Bar
Bass
le - - - i - son,
e - - - - - - - - -
p
Fl.
Ob.
B♭ Cl.
Bsn.
B♭ Tpt.
Hn.
Tbn.
Timp.
Vln I
Vln II
Vla
Vlc
Bass
pp

le - - - - i - son.

le - - - - i - son.

le - - - - i - son.

le - - - - i - son.

le - - - i - son.

le - - - rit. - i - son.

Moderato
♩ = 92

Solo

mp

(with mute)

p (with mute)

p (with mute)

p (with mute)

p (with mute)

rit.

rit.

rit.

rit.

rit.

p

332

17
Sop 1
Sop 2
Alto
Ten
Bar
Bass
17
Fl.
Ob.
B♭ Cl.
Bsn.
17
B♭ Tpt.
Hn.
Tbn.
17
Timp.
17
Vln I
Vln II
Vla
Vlc
Bass

21
Sop 1
Sop 2
Alto
Ten
Bar
Bass
Fl.
Ob.
B♭ Cl.
Bsn.
B♭ Tpt.
Hn.
Tbn.
Timp.
Vln I
Vln II
Vla
Vlc
Bass

25
Sop 1
Sop 2
Alto
Ten
Bar
Bass
Fl.
Ob.
B♭ Cl.
Bsn.
B♭ Tpt.
Hn.
Tbn.
Timp.
Vln I
Vln II
Vla
Vlc
Bass

29
poco rit.
Sop 1
Sop 2
Alto
Ten
Bar
Bass
Fl.
Ob.
B♭ Cl.
Bsn.
B♭ Tpt.
Hn.
Tbn.
Timp.
Vln I
Vln II
Vla
Vlc
Bass
(remove mute)

33
Sop 1
Sop 2
Alto
Ten
Bar
Bass
Fl.
Ob.
B♭ Cl.
Bsn.
B♭ Tpt.
Hn.
Tbn.
Timp.
Vln I
Vln II
Vla
Vlc
Bass

37
Sop 1
Sop 2
Alto
Ten
Bar
Bass
Fl.
Ob.
B♭ Cl.
Bsn.
B♭ Tpt.
Hn.
Tbn.
Timp.
Vln I
Vln II
Vla
Vlc
Bass

41
Sop 1
Sop 2
Alto
Ten
Bar
Bass
Fl.
Ob.
B♭ Cl.
Bsn.
B♭ Tpt.
Hn.
Tbn.
Timp.
Vln I
Vln II
Vla
Vlc
Bass

45
♩= 92 (same tempo)
Sop 1
p
Weep
Sop 2
p
Weep
Alto
Ten
Bar
Bass
45
Fl.
decrescendo
Ob.
decrescendo
p
B♭ Cl.
decrescendo
Bsn.
decrescendo
45
B♭ Tpt.
Hn.
3
3
decrescendo
Tbn.
45
Timp.
45
Vln I
3
p
Vln II
3
p
Vla
3
p
Vlc
3
p
Bass
p

49
Sop 1
we
shall,
weep
we
Sop 2
we
shall,
weep
we
Alto
Ten
Bar
Bass
Fl.
Ob.
B♭ Cl.
Bsn.
B♭ Tpt.
Hn.
Tbn.
Timp.
Vln I
Vln II
Vla
Vlc
Bass

342

57
Sop 1
Sop 2
Alto
weep
we
shall,
3
Ten
Weep
Bar
Bass
Fl.
Ob.
B♭ Cl.
Bsn.
B♭ Tpt.
Hn.
Tbn.
Timp.
Vln I
Vln II
Vla
Vlc
Bass

344

65
Sop 1
Sop 2
Alto
Ten
shall
Bar
Weep
we
shall, weep
Bass
Weep
we
shall, weep
Fl.
Ob.
B♭ Cl.
Bsn.
B♭ Tpt.
Hn.
Tbn.
Timp.
Vln I
Vln II
Vla
Vlc
Bass

69
crescendo
accel.
Faster
♩= 100
Sop 1
Sop 2
Alto
Ten
Bar
Bass
And re - joice
And re - joice
And re -
And re
we shall
And re -
we shall
And re
Fl.
Ob.
B♭ Cl.
Bsn.
B♭ Tpt.
Hn.
Tbn.
Timp.
Vln I
Vln II
Vla
Vlc
Bass

73
Sop 1
with the joy - ful, and re - joice
Sop 2
with the joy - ful, and re - joice
Alto
joice with the joy - ful, re - joice
Ten
joice with the joy - ful, re - joice
Bar
joice with the joy - ful, re joice re joice
Bass
joice with the joy - - ful, re -
Fl.
Ob.
B♭ Cl.
Bsn.
B♭ Tpt.
Hn.
Tbn.
Timp.
Vln I
Vln II
Vla
Vlc
Bass

77
Sop 1
with the joy - - - - - ful, the joy 3 - ful,
Sop 2
with the joy - - - - - ful, the joy - ful,
Alto
re - joice joy ful, joy - ful, the joy - ful,
Ten
re - joice re - joice with the joy 3 -
Bar
with the joy - ful, with the joy 3 -
Bass
joice re - - - - joice with the joy -
Fl.
Ob.
B♭ Cl.
Bsn.
B♭ Tpt.
Hn.
Tbn.
Timp.
Vln I
Vln II
Vla
Vlc
Bass

81
Sop 1
joy - ful, joy - ful, and re - joice
Sop 2
joy - ful, joy - ful, and re - joice
Alto
joy - ful, joy - ful, and re - joice
Ten
ful, joy - ful, joy - ful, and re - joice
Bar
ful, joy - ful, joy - ful, and re - joice
Bass
ful, joy - ful, joy - ful, and re - joice
crescendo
Fl.
Ob.
B♭ Cl.
Bsn.
B♭ Tpt.
Hn.
Tbn.
Timp.
tr
Vln I
Vln II
Vla
Vlc
Bass

85
Sop 1
Sop 2
Alto
Ten
Bar
Bass
Fl.
Ob.
B♭ Cl.
Bsn.
B♭ Tpt.
Hn.
Tbn.
Timp.
Vln I
Vln II
Vla
Vlc
Bass
rit.
ff
mp
with the joy - ful. With all a-ni-mals,
re - joice with joy - ful. With a-ni-mals,
re - joice with the joy - ful, With a-ni-mals,
re - - - - joice with the joy - ful. With
with the joy - ful. With

89
Sop 1
with all a - ni - mals, both tamed
Sop 2
with all a - ni - mals, both tamed
Alto
with all a - ni - mals, both tamed
Ten
with all a - ni - mals, both tamed tamed
Bar
all a - ni - mals, both tamed
Bass
all a - ni - mals, both tamed
Fl.
Ob.
B♭ Cl.
Bsn.
B♭ Tpt.
Hn.
Tbn.
Timp.
Vln I
Vln II
Vla
Vlc
Bass

Requiem VII: Lux perpetua

97
Faster
♩= 108
Sop 1
Sop 2
Alto
Ten
Bar
Bass
mf
with ev' - ry bird with ev' - ry bird with ev' - ry
with ev' - ry bird with ev' - ry bird with ev' - ry
with ev' - ry bird with ev' - ry bird with
with ev' - ry bird with ev' - ry bird with
with ev' - ry bird with
with ev' - ry bird with
Fl.
Ob.
B♭ Cl.
Bsn.
B♭ Tpt.
Hn.
Tbn.
Timp.
Vln I
Vln II
Vla
Vlc
Bass

101
Sop 1
bird
with ev' - ry bird and
Sop 2
bird
with ev' - ry bird and
Alto
ev' - ry bird
with ev' - ry bird and
Ten
ev' - ry bird
with ev' - ry bird and
Bar
ev' - ry bird
with ev' - ry bird and
Bass
ev' - ry bird
with ev' - ry bird and
Fl.
Ob.
B♭ Cl.
Bsn.
B♭ Tpt.
Hn.
Tbn.
Timp.
Vln I
Vln II
Vla
Vlc
Bass

105
Sop 1
fish, in gla - ring sun
Sop 2
fish, in gla - ring sun
Alto
fish, in gla - ring sun gla - ring
Ten
fish, in gla - ring sun gla - ring
Bar
fish, in gla - ring sun
Bass
fish, in gla - ring sun
Fl.
Ob.
B♭ Cl.
Bsn.
B♭ Tpt.
Hn.
Tbn.
Timp.
Vln I
Vln II
Vla
Vlc
Bass

meno mosso
♩= 92
109
rit.
decrescendo
p
Sop 1
Sop 2
Alto
Ten
Bar
Bass
gla - ring sun and un-der a si - - - lent
sun gla - ring sun and un-der a si - - lent
Fl.
Ob.
B♭ Cl.
Bsn.
B♭ Tpt.
Hn.
Tbn.
Timp.
Vln I
Vln II
Vla
Vlc
Bass

113
Sop 1
moon, un - der a si - - - - - lent
Sop 2
moon, un - der a si - - - - - lent
Alto
moon, un - der a si - - - - - lent
Ten
moon, un - der a si - - - - - lent
Bar
moon, un - der a si - - - - - lent
Bass
moon, un - der a si - - - - - lent
Fl.
Ob.
B♭ Cl.
Bsn.
B♭ Tpt.
Hn.
Tbn.
Timp.
Vln I
Vln II
Vla
Vlc
Bass

117
Sop 1
Sop 2
Alto
Ten
Bar
Bass
crescendo
mf
moon,
un - der trees and in the
Fl.
Ob.
B♭ Cl.
Bsn.
B♭ Tpt.
Hn.
Tbn.
Timp.
Vln I
Vln II
Vla
Vlc
Bass

121
Sop 1
o-pen, un - der trees and in the o - pen,
Sop 2
o-pen, un - der trees and in the o - pen,
Alto
o - pen, un - der trees and in the o - pen,
Ten
o - pen, un - der trees and in the o - pen,
Bar
o-pen, un - der trees un - der trees and in the o - pen,
Bass
o-pen, un - der trees un - der trees and in the o - pen,
Fl.
Ob.
B♭ Cl.
Bsn.
B♭ Tpt.
Hn.
Tbn.
Timp.
Vln I
Vln II
Vla
Vlc
Bass

125
Sop 1
in the o - - pen, on high
Sop 2
in the o - - pen, on high
Alto
in the o - pen, on high seas,
Ten
in the o - pen, on high seas,
Bar
in the o - pen, on high
Bass
in the o - pen on high
Fl.
Ob.
B♭ Cl.
Bsn.
B♭ Tpt.
Hn.
Tbn.
Timp.
Vln I
Vln II
Vla
Vlc
Bass

129
Sop 1
seas, high seas, on
Sop 2
seas, high seas, on
Alto
seas, high seas, on
Ten
high seas, high seas,
Bar
high seas, high seas,
Bass
seas, high seas, on
Fl.
Ob.
B♭ Cl.
Bsn.
B♭ Tpt.
Hn.
Tbn.
Timp.
Vln I
Vln II
Vla
Vlc
Bass

133
Sop 1
high seas and in deep
Sop 2
high seas and in deep
Alto
high seas and in deep
Ten
high seas, and in deep
Bar
high seas and in deep
Bass
high seas, and in deep
Fl.
Ob.
B♭ Cl.
Bsn.
B♭ Tpt.
Hn.
Tbn.
Timp.
Vln I
Vln II
Vla
Vlc
Bass

137
Sop 1
Sop 2
Alto
Ten
Bar
Bass
Fl.
Ob.
B♭ Cl.
Bsn.
B♭ Tpt.
Hn.
Tbn.
Timp.
Vln I
Vln II
Vla
Vlc
Bass
rit.
a tempo
pp
dales
by
day

141
Sop 1
Sop 2
Alto
Ten
Bar
Bass
and night
mp
on
Fl.
Ob.
B♭ Cl.
Bsn.
B♭ Tpt.
Hn.
Tbn.
Timp.
Vln I
Vln II
Vla
Vlc
Bass

145
Sop 1
earth and in hea - - - ven, on
Sop 2
earth, and in hea - - - ven, on
Alto
earth and in hea - - - ven, on
Ten
earth and in hea - - - ven,
Bar
earth and in hea - - - ven,
Bass
earth and in hea - - - ven,
Fl.
Ob.
B♭ Cl.
Bsn.
B♭ Tpt.
Hn.
Tbn.
Timp.
Vln I
Vln II
Vla
mp
Vlc
mp
Bass

149
Sop 1
earth and in hea - - - - - - - -
Sop 2
earth and in hea - - - - - - - -
Alto
earth and in hea - - - - - - - -
Ten
earth and in hea - - - - - - - -
Bar
earth and in hea - - - - - - - -
Bass
earth and in hea - - - - - - - -
149
Fl.
Ob.
B♭ Cl.
Bsn.
149
B♭ Tpt.
Hn.
Tbn.
149
Timp.
149
Vln I
Vln II
Vla
Vlc
Bass

153
Sop 1
ven, on earth, on
Sop 2
ven, on earth, on
Alto
ven, earth,
Ten
ven, earth,
Bar
ven, earth,
Bass
ven, earth,
Fl.
Ob.
B♭ Cl.
Bsn.
B♭ Tpt.
Hn.
Tbn.
Timp.
Vln I
Vln II
Vla
Vlc
Bass

157
Sop 1
Sop 2
Alto
Ten
Bar
Bass
crescendo
earth and in hea - - - - ven, on earth and in
earth and in hea - - - - ven, on earth and in
earth and in hea - - - - - - - - ven, in
earth and hea - - - - - - - - ven, in
earth and hea - - - - - - - - ven, in
earth and hea - - - - - - - - ven, in
Fl.
Ob.
B♭ Cl.
Bsn.
B♭ Tpt.
Hn.
Tbn.
Timp.
Vln I
Vln II
Vla
Vlc
Bass

Andante ♩= 84 freely
161
rit. mf pp
Sop 1
Sop 2
Alto
Ten
Bar
Bass
hea - - - - - - - - ven,
Do - na
hea - - - - - - - - ven.
Fl.
Ob.
B♭ Cl.
Bsn.
B♭ Tpt.
Hn.
Tbn.
Timp.
Vln I
Vln II
Vla
Vlc
Bass

165
Sop 1
Sop 2
Alto
Ten
Bar
Bass
no - bis re - qui - em. Do - na
p
Fl.
Ob.
B♭ Cl.
Bsn.
B♭ Tpt.
Hn.
Tbn.
Timp.
Vln I
Vln II
Vla
Vlc
Bass

169
Sop 1
Sop 2
Alto
Ten
Bar
Bass
no - - - bis re - qui - em.
mp
Do - na
Do - - -
no - bis re - qui - em.
Fl.
Ob.
B♭ Cl.
Bsn.
B♭ Tpt.
Hn.
Tbn.
Timp.
Vln I
Vln II
Vla
Vlc
Bass

173
rit.
Sop 1
no - bis, do - na no - bis re - qui -
Sop 2
na do - na no - bis re - qui -
Alto
na do - na no - bis re - qui -
Ten
na do - na no - bis re - qui -
Bar
na do - na no - bis re - qui -
Bass
na do - na no - bis re - qui -
173
Fl.
Ob.
B♭ Cl.
Bsn.
173
B♭ Tpt.
Hn.
Tbn.
173
Timp.
173
Vln I
Vln II
Vla
Vlc
Bass

177
All soprano 1 and soloist
Sop 1
Sop 2
Alto
Ten
Bar
Bass
All baritones and soloist
em.
Et
lux
per - - - - -
mf
Fl.
Ob.
B♭ Cl.
Bsn.
B♭ Tpt.
Hn
Tbn.
Timp.
Vln I
Vln II
Vla
Vlc
Bass

181
Sop 1
pe - - - tu - a, et lux
Sop 2
pe - - - tu - a, et lux
Alto
pe - - - tu - a, et lux
Ten
pe - - - tu - a, et lux
Bar
pe - - - tu - a, et lux
Bass
pe - - - tu - a, et lux
Fl.
Ob.
B♭ Cl.
Bsn.
B♭ Tpt.
Hn.
Tbn.
Timp.
Vln I
Vln II
Vla
Vlc
Bass

meno mosso
♩= 84
185
Sop 1
Sop 2
Alto
Ten
Bar
Bass
per - - - pe - - tu - a, et
per - - - pe - - tu - a et
per - - - pe - - tu - a et
per - - - pe - tu - a et
per - - - pe - tu - a et
per - - pe - tu - a et
mp
Fl.
Ob.
B♭ Cl.
Bsn.
B♭ Tpt.
Hn.
Tbn.
Timp.
Vln I
Vln II
Vla
Vlc
Bass

376

377

197
rit.
Slower
♩= 72
Sop 1
Sop 2
Alto
Ten
Bar
Bass
Fl.
Ob.
B♭ Cl.
Bsn.
B♭ Tpt.
Hn.
Tbn.
Timp.
Vln I
Vln II
Vla
Vlc
Bass
crescendo
decrescendo
mp
mf
f
p
tr

Latin Text of <u>Weep with Those Who Weep: a Requiem</u>

The texts are taken from the traditional Latin requiem.

I Dona nobis requiem

Dona nobis requiem
Et lux perpetua luceat

II Eleison

Eleison

III Dies Irae

Sale nobis, fons pietatis

Dies irae, dies illa
Solvet saeclum in favilla

Lacrimosa dies illa
Qua resurget ex favilla
Judicandus homo reus

IV De profundo lacu

De poenis inferni
et de profundo lacu
"miserere!" supplicamus
libera nos de ore leonis
ne cadamus in obscurum.

V Hosanna in excelsis

Pleni sunt coeli et terra
gloria magnifica.
Hosanna in excelsis!

VI Qui tollit peccata mundi?

Agnus Dei, qui tollit
Peccata mundi,
Dona nobis requiem

Qui tollit peccata mundi?
Dona nobis requiem

VII Lux perpetua

Eleison

Dona nobis requiem
Et lux perpetua luceat

I Grant us rest

Grant us rest
And let eternal light shine

II Have mercy

Have mercy

III Day of wrath

Save us, source of pity

That day of wrath, that day
Will dissolve the world in ashes

Tearful will be that day,
on which from the ash arises
the guilty human to be judged.

IV From the bottomless pit

From the pains of hell
and from the bottomless pit
we beg and cry "mercy!"
deliver us from the jaws of the lion
and let us not fall into darkness

V Hosanna in the highest

Heaven and earth are full
of magnificent glory.
Hosanna in the highest!

VI Who takes away the sins of the world?

Lamb of God who takes away
The sins of the world,
Grant us rest

Who will take away the sins of the world?
Grant us rest

VII Eternal Light

Have mercy

Grant us rest
and let the eternal light shine

www.ingramcontent.com/pod-product-compliance
Lightning Source LLC
Chambersburg PA
CBHW062033090426

42740CB00016B/2889